TEEN BOYS' COMEDIC MONOLOGUES THAT ARE ACTUALLY FUNNY

TEEN BOYS' COMEDIC MONOLOGUES THAT ARE ACTUALLY FUNNY

Edited by

ALISHA GADDIS

APPLAUSE
THEATRE & CINEMA BOOKS
An Imprint of Hal Leonard Corporation

Published in 2015 by Applause Theatre & Cinema Books
An Imprint of Hal Leonard Corporation
7777 West Bluemound Road
Milwaukee, WI 53213

Trade Book Division Editorial Offices
33 Plymouth St., Montclair, NJ 07042

Printed in the United States of America

Book design by UB Communications

Library of Congress Cataloging-in-Publication Data

Teen boys' comedic monologues that are actually funny / edited by Alisha Gaddis.
   pages cm
ISBN 978-1-4803-9679-1 (pbk.)
1. Monologues—Juvenile literature. 2. Acting—Auditions—Juvenile literature. 3. Comedy sketches—Juvenile literature. I. Gaddis, Alisha, editor.
PN2080.T485 2015
812'.0450817—dc23
                        2015018241

www.applausebooks.com

Contents

Introduction

Guys—you are holding in your hands something awesome. Something that is fresh, edgy, hip, and FUNNY! Something that is going to help you book the part that is already YOURS for the taking.

You, teen boys, are not like the teen boys of your grandfathers or your fathers or your father's father's father's neighbor's time. You are you. You have access to all things NOW—technology, sports, gaming, first love, travel, world domination! But you already know this, don't you? #YOLO was the past, and this book is the present.

You need something hysterical, raw, real, and YOU for those auditions where you are supposed to be funny, actually funny.

This book is the answer to your needs. It was written by people who are funny for a living: stand-up comics, comedy writers, and directors living in Los Angeles and New York (and a few places in between). These writers want you to land the role, steal the show, make them laugh, and live your dreams.

Because that is what it is all about anyway.

Alisha Gaddis

Forever 41

Alisha Gaddis

RICKY, 15

RICKY *is on the sidewalk outside of his house yelling back to his mom, who is in their running '96 Honda Accord. He starts to walk away, but then walks back to scold her.*

RICKY   No, Mom—I am not getting in the car.

NO.

NOOOO!!! I don't care if school is over four miles away. I will walk on my own two feet and keep my dignity in tact.

Why? Really? You want to know why?! . . .

I don't think you can handle the truth, Ma. But here is—raw and ready.

My friends call you a MILF.

A MILF, MOM!!!

Do you even know what that means, Mom? MILF. It means "Mom, I'd Like to *F*-word-that-I-would-rather-not-say-in-front-of-my-own-mother."

Mom—I am fifteen and just getting my foot in with girls and you are what the other boys are talking about and it is gross and I will not stand for it!!

[*Beat.*]

It IS your fault mom! 120,000 percent it is! Look where you shop! It is not called Forever 41—it is called Forever 21. Like you want to be 21 FOREVER. Look at you, Mom—you have on a tube dress. It is 8:00 a.m. for god's sakes. Why do you look like you just came from a One Direction concert at the crack of dawn?!

I saw how you heated up the Hot Pockets for the guys the other day—you were all laughing and smiling and wearing those weird really short cut-off shorts that you ALWAYS put on when Gabe the UPS driver has something to deliver. You had THOSE shorts on, Mom. And you bent down to get the Hot Pockets out of the stove and everyone was looking to see if they could see your twat!

[*Beat.*]

Don't gasp, Mom—you did this to me! You made me say "twat"!

I think you like it. You like the attention! You know they are watching and you giggle. DISGUSTING. You are my mother. You birthed me. You could have birthed them, too. They are THAT much younger than you!

I can't take it anymore. Yes—you are still attractive and I know you had me at a young age and you still have the goods and you need to feel like a woman and not just a mother and blah blah blah, but can' t you just for ONCE put on a cardigan, some slacks, and maybe some I'm-still-cool Converse sneakers instead of a low-cut shirt and miniskirt with high stripper heels?!! JUST ONCE!!

[*Beat.*]

Mom—don't cry. I'm sorry, I just . . .

You're my mom and I don't like it. I know I am the man of the house now, and I had to take a stand. You aren't just embarrassing me, but you are embarrassing yourself.

Now, let's wipe away that blue eye makeup running down your face with tears, and maybe after school I can take you to the mall.

Young and Brave
Leo DiCaprio

Carla Cackowski

LEO DICAPRIO, 14

LEO *is 14. And very confident. He is auditioning for a TV show.*

LEO Yes ma'am, I'm ready to slate. I've never been more ready for anything in my life. Shall I take my mark? Oh, you don't need to show me. I know where it is. This isn't my first time at the dog and pony show, know what I mean?

[*The boy takes his mark and smiles into the camera.*]

Hello. My name is Leonardo DiCaprio. I'm fourteen years old. I'm going to book this role.

Pardon me? You'd like me to do it again? Are you sure? It really seemed like I nailed it. Ohhh, I see. It was your fault. Not mine. Makes sense. I don't mess things up. No need to apologize. No big deal. Takes more to distract me than a camera operator forgetting to turn on the camera.

[*He stares intensely into the camera.*]

Hello. My name is Leonardo DiCaprio. You can call me Leo. I'm auditioning for *Huckleberry Finn*. I'm the best person for this role. You want me.

[*He relaxes on hearing "Cut."*]

Yeah, that was pretty good, wasn't it?

[LEO *smooths out his hair.*]

Question before I read for you. *Huckleberry Finn* was written in the late 1800s. I think that may be a little outdated for a television show. How about I play him like he was born in the late 1900s? You know, closer to when I was born. My life has been pretty interesting so far. I think Ol' Been Around Forever Huck could use a fresh perspective. Now, I know it's a bold choice, but nobody reaps the benefits of playing this game of life if we play it safe, right?

Yes, I knew you'd see things my way. I have very good instincts. Like a hunter. Or a fox. Or a hunter hunting a fox. Or a fox hiding from a hunter. Either way, I'm on top of things.

Yes, I'm ready. I'm always ready. Whatever you throw at me, I hit it out of the park. Just say, "action."

[LEO *takes in a deep breath and looks into the camera, a charming smile on his lips.*]

That's right, buddy boy, my name's Huck Finn. And I'm a winner.

[LEO *relaxes as he hears, "Cut."*]

Thank you, yes, I thought that was very good too. I hope it's okay that I changed the lines a bit. Or entirely. I just thought you'd want a natural read on the character and I couldn't say any of the lines the way Mark Twain wrote them. No disrespect, I see what the writer was going for—I just think my way is better.

Glad you agree. Would you like me to do something else for you before I leave to meet my seventeen-year-old hot-bod model girlfriend? No? I got the part! Makes sense.

You haven't even sent the producers my tape yet, and I got the part. Yeah, you're right—no need to see anyone else, they would pick me anyway. Some people are just born under a lucky star. They're handsome, talented, and magnetic. I am one of these people. You won't be sorry you chose me, Leonardo DiCaprio. I make everything better.

Transition

Alessandra Rizzotti

TOM, 14

TOM, *age 14, who identifies as Teresa, is about to come out to his drama club friend as transsexual. Teresa is femme already, and her friends assume she's a gay male, but Teresa has always been a girl, since she was little. This is a big moment for her.*

TOM   Sarah, you know how we're prepping for Nationals this year? I figured I didn't want to compete with a duet with you like last year. Don't get me wrong, I love working with you. I just want to end high school on a big note.

Can you listen? Seriously. Don't get all hissy fitty on me. I've been working on a play about a guy who doesn't want to come out to his parents. It's sweet. Sensual. Pretty PG. Almost like *Blossom* meets *Glee*. Remember the floating bag in *American Beauty*? It's like the tone of that.

No Sarah, I'm not gay. I just think this play is probably the easiest way to express myself to drama club this year.

Because, I dunno. There's no other way to talk about this. Sarah, I want to tell you something. Can you listen?

Why are you so excited? What I'm about to tell you might weird you out and I'm nervous. Stop smiling. Okay. Here goes. I always knew I liked dressing up in women's clothes since I was two years old, but I'm starting to realize that that's not gay . . . that's something else. I've been looking it up on Google and I am realizing that I really identify as a woman. O-M-G. Can you listen? Because I want you to be the first person I told. You really helped me that one time when you and I were putting on makeup for fun, and I just realized in that moment how natural and good that felt. It felt like myself. Because when I put on skater shorts and baggy shirts, I feel like I'm outside my skin.

Sarah, no, you can't tell anyone. I sorta need to do this on my own. I was thinking that I could do it at the end of the play. My mom and dad don't know. Honestly, they would probably be fine with it. I once found heels in my dad's car once, so either he is having an affair or he dresses up like a woman too. And as for my mom, she knows I wear her lipstick in my room and dance to Diana Ross. I mean, she sometimes wants to join. So it's no big deal on my family end. I just sorta want to be able to come out to all the kids at school in a really dignified sorta way.

Why? Because it would be freeing. I don't want to start my life as a whole new person in college; I want to be the person

I've always wanted to be, starting now. Why can't you understand that?

We're best friends, Sarah. I don't like you that way. Shut up. You didn't think I liked you, did you? We're soul mates. That's a different kind of love. O-M-G. Are you serious? My sexuality is fluid. I like boys and girls, just not you. I swear I didn't mean to hurt you this way. Sarah, I thought we were so close because we were just best friends. No! I thought you wanted to wait till marriage to kiss and have sex, not for ME. Ah! This is so confusing. I didn't mean to confuse you.

I love you, but not in a sexual way. How did this become about us and not me? You always do that. Can't you listen for once? Can't you hear me out? Are we not going to be friends anymore? O-M-G. I thought you were a Christian liberal. One day when the world isn't so bigoted, I'll be able to be myself.

What? I thought you were mad. Well I'm not in love back. I'm sorry. This conversation just made me asexual.

The Case for a Later Curfew

Chris Quintos

HENRY, 15 to 16

HENRY, *a high school sophomore, initiates after-dinner negotiations with his mother for a later curfew. He was raised by lawyers and knows that the best way to a win an argument is with a well-structured case.*

HENRY   Look, Mom. Just try to put yourself in my shoes. For, like, five minutes, can you, like, let me walk you through, step by step, why it's important to extend my curfew. Just five minutes of your time, please. Let me begin by saying that you look beautiful tonight, and dinner was absolutely delicious.

[*Clears throat.*]

Mom, thank you for being here tonight. I would like to begin with point number 1: I'm not a freshman anymore. I know what you're going to say, "You're just a sophomore,

Henry." But here's the thing that you fail to see. You're just not there on the ground anymore. High school was so long ago for you! BUT you don't look a day over twenty-five! And I mean that. Freshmen are basically babies. They are FRESH out of the womb of baby school. You see what I did there? And me? I'm just not that person anymore. I've lived, no, *clawed* my way through one whole academic year of the high school trenches. I know who the cool kids on campus are, I recognize their names, their faces. I know their interests. Heck, I know that there ARE cool kids, and an entire hierarchy! My eyes are WIDE open, Mom. I'm not a baby anymore.

Which brings me to my second point. I will never—and I truly mean this—NEVER make it to cool kid status if I have to be home by 10:00 p.m. That's when things start happening. That's when the action gets good! All parent-approved, good, wholesome action, of course! At 10:00 p.m., all the kids, cool or not, are just getting out of football/basketball/volleyball games. That's when the parents bid adieu to their beloved—and TRUSTWORTHY—children and let them run around until 1:00 a.m.

Now, now, please don't interrupt me. I'm not asking for a 1:00 a.m. curfew. Come on, Mom. I wasn't born yesterday. All I'm saying is that 1:00 a.m. is the time most teens are due at home—if they're due at all! Some kids don't even have curfews.

And, I'm NOT saying that, either. But what I am saying,
Dear Mother, is that 10:00 p.m. is completely unreasonable.
You're tying my hands, Mom. Can't you see that?

Think about it this way. You've done a great—no,
EXEMPLARY—job of raising a responsible kid! Right?
Don't answer that. Let me just keep going. You have taught
me right from wrong. I know that drugs are bad. And sex is
bad—unless it's with the right person! And lying is bad and
being bad is bad. I get it! I totally get it, but now it's time to
take the training wheels off and let's see if this baby can ride!
Let's see if all your hard work . . . works!

How about this—we try it, one weekend. Maybe
homecoming weekend? And we just do a trial run of a
midnight curfew. If that works well, maybe—and all I'm
saying is MAYBE—it gets extended to 12:30 if I can
consistently prove myself to be worthy of your trust.
Whaddya think, Mama? Also, did I mention I love you?

The Surprise

Jessica Glassberg

LEON, 18

LEON, *with a large backpack, hops into a taxi.*

LEON Hi—four-oh-five Sycamore, please? Between Main and Third. [*Looking at the driver's GPS.*]

Wow, that's a cool GPS. That's great that it shows you a picture of the Anderson dorm.

I'm visiting my girlfriend. Ali. Her name's Ali. Well, it's Alison, but I'm sure you figured that out. It's a pretty common name.

[*Pulling up a picture on his phone of a girl, 18, and showing the driver.*]

Cute, right? I am so excited to see her. It's been three months. She decided to go to college out of state. I stayed in, and we were so nervous about the whole long-distance thing, but I knew we'd make it work. I'm surprising her for our two-year anniversary.

[*A beat. Then,*]

Man, I'm nervous. It's just so exciting to see the girl I'm probably gonna marry. I actually thought about asking her this weekend. But we're only eighteen. We have time. Well, that's what my mom says. I would have proposed to Ali the night we met. She's just so perfect.

[*Flipping through pictures on his phone.*]

Oh, this was the night before she left for orientation. She's such a cute crier. But I promised that I'd call her every night. And I do. We always have our seven o'clock date. We watch *Seinfeld* reruns together while we talk about our day.

[*He holds up another picture of Ali.*]

Ha, this is us on our first Skype call. We didn't have a great connection, so now we just stick to talking on the phone. It feels more classically romantic. She always answers after three rings. It's really cute. Well, when she answers it's after three rings. She started having Netflix nights on Tuesdays with some people in her dorm. So, we moved our seven o'clock date back to six, but then she would be picking up dinner to bring to Netflix night, so sometimes we just skip Tuesdays and I leave her a goodnight voicemail. And on Thursdays she has her econ study group. I really wish I could be there to tutor her. But she said her TA, Chris—don't worry, it's short for Christine—well, she has been great and gives her extra help after office hours. She lives in her dorm, which is really convenient. And Fridays and Saturdays we just decided would be too tough to talk at seven because we're both getting ready to go out. I mean, I don't go out too much, but there are some cool guys in my dorm and we get together to play cards and stuff. I don't want to go to parties and grind up on other women. It's just weird. But I want to make sure Ali gets the full college experience, plus she just likes dancing with the girls in her dorm.

[*Looking at the GPS.*]

Oh, only two blocks away. Do you think I should call? I should totally call to throw her off.

[*He dials. . . . Says to driver:*]

Voicemail.

[*Into phone:*]

Hey Sugarbear, it's Honey Bee. I was just thinking about you and wishing we could be together today.

[*Stifling a laugh. Then, in an overly dramatic tone*]

Oh, if only there was some way for us to be together. Well, give me a call back so we can . . .

[*Noticing something out his window.*]

There she is!

[*Calling out his window:*]

Ali!

[*To the driver:*]

I don't think she heard me. Oh . . . and there's Chris.

[*Out his window:*]

Hey . . . Ali!

[*To the driver:*]

Wait . . . are they . . . Is she kissing her?

[*To the driver:*]

I'm so glad she made such a good friend.

[*A beat. Then,*]

That's a long kiss.

[*A beat. Then,*]

. . . A really long kiss.

[*Out his window:*]

Hey, Ali! It's me . . . Honey Bee . . . Buzzzzzz . . .

[*To the driver:*]

Hey! Where are you going? Why are you rerouting us back to the airport?!?!

Didn't Get the Job

Alessandra Rizzotti

DONALD, 18

DONALD *looks disappointed. He starts talking to his dad, who is in the other room.*

DONALD   Dad, I just wanted to tell you I didn't get the job at McDonald's. It's not that I'm not talented, you see. It's that they don't like my ideas. I'm "too creative," they say. Like they didn't like the idea to mix Mountain Dew and Sprite and Orange Pop for a special soda drink. Or to mix the ketchup and ranch, which is so good, by the way, because it's way better than that special sauce at In-N-Out. It has more of a kick, ya know? I'm just too ahead of my time. It's a shame they don't see that.

You know how in seventh grade I used to sell grilled cheeses outside of reggae concerts and I'd get all the stoners to buy me out? I was an entrepreneur. I knew an opportunity when I saw one. I was also an inventor. You remember when you helped me patent that backpack that was really a front-and-backpack? I mean, it was genius. It had potential—you know that, Dad. I have potential.

Anyways, Dad, I applied for three other great jobs today. I know something will come around. I'm ready for it. I just know I can be a manager at Walgreens at least. They gotta see that even without a college degree, I'm sharp. I got people skills, even though I don't know how to price stuff or do money stuff.

[*He sits on the couch and turns on the TV.*]

Is the game on? I don't want to miss it. The Red Sox have to win. I've been thinking about it all day. I know they have potential, just like I do. World Series is totally in their future.

Hey, what do I tell Tracy? She wanted to go out and celebrate because I made her think I was gonna get the McDonald's thing, but now it's just like, I dunno? I just feel like I should make sure I have a job before I have negative five dollars in the piggy bank, you know what I mean?

[*He sighs.*]

I don't mean to keep disappointing you, Dad. I want to get the rent in order for next week, but it doesn't seem like it will happen if Tracy and I have to get the baby carriage and the stuff for the nursery tomorrow. Thanks for being a lifesaver this whole time, by the way.

[*He looks at the TV.*]

No fucking way! They're losing again. I can't stand how much they just never satisfy me, and yet I keep coming back like a sucker. Reminds me of Tracy. Ha-hah. Dad, can I have a beer and a hot dog on a stick? It's been a hard day.

[*He opens the can.*]

Thanks for understanding, Dad. Man, how will I be as good a dad as you?

Dude, I'm a Dad

Jessica Glassberg

DAX, 16

DAX *is a 16-year-old father, holding his newborn daughter for the first time. He stares at her, shell-shocked.*

DAX [*Beat.*] So, Madeline . . . What's up?

[*Awaiting a response.*]

Looks like I'm gonna be your dad, Dude. Well, I guess I already am your dad. And you're not a dude . . . a dude-ette? I dunno . . . I dunno a lot of things. For most stuff, ask your mom I guess. She's pretty smart.

[*A beat. Then,*]

Don't tell her I told you that.

[DAX *looks at his little girl. Beat.*]

I was really hoping you were gonna be a boy.

[*Beat. Then, sternly,*]

Don't post naked pictures of yourself online! No sex until
you're thirty!

[*Mockingly,*]

This is your father speaking!

[*Laughing, then,*]

Yeah, a boy woulda been better.

[*Covering,*]

Well, not better. You're . . . fine. I think it just would be
easier. Girls make me uncomfortable. But it's weird—I'm
not sweating and my hands aren't shaking with you. Don't
get me wrong, I'm nervous as all hell. Maybe I just know if
my hands shake too much, I'll drop you. I don't know much
about babies, but I know you shouldn't drop 'em.

[DAX *looks into his daughter's eyes.*]

You have Carly's . . . your mom's . . . eyes. Your eyes are
really blue. Like, really blue. Most newborn babies' eyes are
gray. See, I just taught ya something. I read that in a book.
Oh, and don't tell your mom that I read the baby books;
she'll want me to read other stuff. I hate reading. I probably
shouldn't say that to you. I'm supposed to tell you to read,
and do your homework and not eat paste and be boring. But
ya know what? Paste tastes pretty good. And if you don't
want to read, you don't have to. And if you don't feel like

going to school, don't go! And if you want to spend the summer smoking weed on the beach with your friends instead of getting a job, go for it! Have fun! Get laid!

[DAX's *self-satisfied smile turns to concern.*]

Shit.

[*Then, realizing . . .*]

Oh, sorry for saying "shit" . . . I did it again. Shit. Sorry. I just . . . I don't want you to be a burnout. I want you to go to Harvard and shit. Sorry . . . guess I gotta work on that. But you've gotta be a doctor or a lawyer or something. I dunno. I'm not . . . I'm just not ready to be the man of the house. Any house. Even if that house is the room on top of the garage of your grandparents' house. How am I supposed to tell you what to do, when all I've done is make mistakes?

[DAX *kisses his daughter on the head.*]

But you're no mistake. And I want to make sure you never ever feel like one.

[*Then,*]

C'mon, let's go score some free Jell-o.

Feeling Suicidal

Alessandra Rizzotti

CHRIS, 16 to 18

CHRIS *sits in a therapist's office.*

CHRIS   Derek broke up with me. He said he felt like I didn't love him enough, but I swear I do. It's just gay drama. I don't know what he's even talking about, because two days ago, I saw him with Terrence, you know, my best friend, the one I talked about in our last session, and they were flirting back and forth, singing *Rent* songs together! So I think it's more like he just wants to fool around. Which is, whatever—I don't need that. I could eat a Big Mac and it would be the same sort of unhealthy bullshit.

I know we were only together for six months, but I felt so lonely the day it happened, so I acted out and I went to the Korean spa down the street. And you know, sometimes the men there, they get aggressive. Which is surprising since their dicks are so tiny. I was offered some kinda pill. I don't know what it was. Probably Molly, or maybe some acupuncture herbal stuff. But I took it, and after about thirty minutes, I felt so dizzy, but free at the same time, like *Rosemary's Baby*. It was like everything felt outside my body. Every sensation was fuzzy and warm and it was like not stressful, at all, anymore. I called myself a Carebear to some guy in the corner. And he was this like small Asian dude that didn't speak English, so I bet he was like, "what are you saying?"

I was just feeling like I could conquer the world, so I forgot about Derek and I hooked up with another random Asian guy who had I think an even smaller dick. It was without condoms. It was scary because I didn't even know his name, but at the same time, I didn't care. I really, really didn't care. It was as if I could just die at that moment because why not live it up, right?

I walked home, feeling even lonelier. Like bad lonely. Like the time my mom left me alone for a week at home without any money for groceries and all I ate was corn chips. And so, I felt like I couldn't survive. So if I couldn't survive, why not give up, right? Right then and there? I just had these persistent thoughts of wanting to die. Wanting to just end things. I looked through the medicine cabinet, but all I could find was my mom's Midol and her birth control, so I swear. O-M-G. I was about to take all the Midol and birth control, just to see what it would do. You know, because maybe all the lady hormones would kill me, you know? But, after I took them, I just felt sick, so I threw up all over myself, then peed myself and I swear, I didn't even want to change my clothes. So I slept in my nastiness. I slept in my mess. Being in throw up and pee was like dying, but not.

I imagine if I were to actually kill myself, I'd be way more elegant about it. I'd probably wear a silk robe, put on some Gloria Estefan, and drink myself to sleep with some sort of pills. I'd have to do research on it. Do you think I need to go to the hospital? I mean, I worry that what if, one day, I'm playing Gloria Estefan, and I just have the urge? What would I do? How do I remind myself that I am worth living and breathing?

Are you shitting me? Meditation doesn't work, doc. I'm too creative for that shit. I'll just dance it off, I guess. It seems like the only coping mechanism I have is to be an artist. But seriously, is there medicine I can take for this? I don't know if I can be alone right now. I have to go to ANOTHER doctor to get medicine? What a waste of time. I swear to god, this whole psych industry is just a bunch of bullshit. You just want all my money . . . I know I don't pay for my sessions, but if I was rich, I would. And I'm going to be, doc. I'm going to be a pop star, just you wait.

The Other *Hamlet*

Derek Heeren

MICHAEL, 18

MICHAEL *is auditioning for a revival of* Noises Off! *which is rumored to be headed to Off-Broadway after its run here in Cleveland.*

MICHAEL   [*Speaking to the audience, overly excited.*] First, I just want to say, I'm really excited to be here. You guys are so awesome. And I love this play. The first time I saw it was in third grade—it's probably one of my favorites of all time. In act 2, when . . . Okay, okay, sorry. I'll get started. I'm going to be performing a piece from *Hamlet*.

[*Beat. Getting into character. He holds out his hand as if holding something.*
Breaking character. To audience—referring to his imaginary object.]

By the way, this is a skull.

[*Getting back into character.*
Breaking character again. To audience—pointing at the ground.]

Oh, and we're in a graveyard and that's a grave. Right there.
So, skull . . . and grave—oh, and I'm talking to Horatio.
Who is standing behind you. You, yeah. Actually, why don't
I just make you Horatio? Okay.

[*Getting back into character. Breaking character.*]

Oh, and it doesn't matter yet, but it's April. And there was
just a late snow. But it's melting off a little bit. But it's still
cold. So, this is a skull, this is a grave, you're Horatio, it's
April, and it's cold because it just snowed.

[*Shivers. Back into character.*
Breaking character, frustrated. To audience.]

Sorry, sorry. I forgot to say that this isn't Shakespeare's
Hamlet. This is from a short film I wrote named *Hamlet*
about an undertaker in a small town, which is also called a
"hamlet." This hamlet is actually Washington. Not the
capital, though—Washington, the hamlet. And my character
is also Hamlet. Hamlet Jones. So, skull, grave, Horatio,
April, snow, cold, Washington hamlet, Hamlet Jones.

[*Back in character.*
Breaking character and breaking down, to audience.]

This isn't going how I imagined. I'm all . . . in my head. I
usually do Felix from the *Odd Couple*, but Mr. Coogan said
that everyone does Neil Simon and you'd be sick of it and I
should pick something you've never heard before, and I can't

imagine you'd've heard this, right? Mr. Coogan is my
theater teacher. He's kind of a character actor. You may have
seen him. He's on those mattress commercials; he's like the
big heart and he says, "Have a heart!" And he does a
little . . . dance. It doesn't matter—why am I talking about
that? Unless you know him. Do you know him? Of course
you don't know him! He's nobody—why did I listen to him?
This is horrible. Let me just start. Let me start!

[*Beat.*]

I forgot the first line! You screwed me, Mr. Coogan! You . . .
I have to go.

[*Storms off. Slinks back.*]

Can I try my Odd Couple monologue instead? I feel like
you'd really like that.

The Fourteen-Foot Scarf

Cooper McHatton

HENRY WALLACE, 15

HENRY *paces in front of a couch while on the phone with his grandmother. He holds a scarf in one hand, examining it carefully.*

HENRY   Grandma, this is a great scarf. All the right colors. In the right order. But I was wondering, could you make it about ten feet longer?

Yes, I know that seems too long.

Yes, I know four feet will keep me plenty warm, but I want it the length of the Fourth Doctor's scarf.

No, not your doctor . . . Doctor Who.

I'm not asking you which doctor, I'm telling you, like Doctor Who. Um, I can see you're confused here. I asked for a long scarf so I could look like the Doctor.

Uh, yes, Grandma, I am sure your doctor doesn't wear a fourteen-foot-long scarf. I don't want to look like your doctor, I want to look like the Fourth Doctor. It's a TV show, Grandma.

No, it's not for a costume. It's for cosplay.

I know you're making this scarf as a gift.

Yes, I thank you for not charging me.

No, it doesn't cost to play—it's not "cost-play," it's "cosplay."

Yeah, I'm not sure of the difference either, but it's not a costume. It's . . .?

Well, people my age DO still wear costumes. At Comic-Con there are people of all ages wearing cosplay.

Buying comics is not a con. It's "con" for "convention."

It's huge! Like over a hundred thousand people every year go there.

Sure, thousands of dollars spent on comics sounds like a con, but it's not! They are really valuable! It's art!

No, Grandma, it's not childish.

Yes, I know my room is covered in LEGO, but that's because I'm an AFOL.

No, not "a fool," Grandma . . . It's an abbreviation for Adult Fan of LEGO . . . successful adults all over the world work in LEGO.

Yes, I know I'm a teenager . . . you know what, never mind. Can you just add ten feet onto the scarf?

Prius Convertible

Kathy S Yamamoto

ANTHONY, 15

ANTHONY, *almost 16, is looking forward to his birthday in a little over a week. He's conspiring with his best friend, Allan, on what he thinks his birthday present from his parents will be.*

ANTHONY Bro. Bro, bro, bro. I have big news. Probably the biggest news you'll ever hear in your life. Ever. You know how on Tuesday, I'm getting my learner's permit? And you know how my birthday is next Wednesday? Well, I'm pretty sure that my parents got me a car.

Think about all the dope things we can do once I have my car. We could drive to the game store, we could drive to soccer practice, we could drive to your house. We could drive pretty much anywhere we wanted. I mean, we could even drive to school, but like, why would we wanna do that?

I bet they bought me a green car. They know green is my favorite color. Shut up Allen, blue was my favorite color when I was a baby. I'm almost an adult now. And as an adult, my favorite color is green. Shut up, Allen, adults definitely have favorite colors—haven't you ever seen *Breaking Bad*? Well, you should watch it because it's a great show, but one of the supporting characters' favorite colors is purple, and she's definitely an adult. Don't worry, I didn't spoil anything for you.

Listen, I know they bought me a car! Just trust me! I walked in on them talking last night about how they were so proud of me, and then how the Prius gets great mileage. I know the Prius isn't my first choice in car, either, but it's a car!!! Didn't your parents just get a Prius? Isn't it dope? You're parents were just over telling my parents about how dope it was.

No man, there is no way that I overheard my parents talking about *your* parents' Prius. Why would they also be talking about how proud of me they were? Duh. Look, I'll show you. Every year they hide my birthday present in the garage. They think I don't know. I bet you anything that a brand-new Prius will be sitting there, probably with a big bow like they have in car commercials. Or maybe they'll put the bow on Tuesday. My mom might not have had time to buy the bow yet, you know she's super busy at work.

[ANTHONY *opens the door to the garage. There is no car there.*]

Don't be a dummy, Allan. I'm still getting my Prius! Look, there's a box here. I bet you that in the box is car keys—to my new green Prius. It makes so much sense! They probably

want to drive it up to me to build suspense. I'm going to
have to practice looking surprised. How does this look?
Maybe a little less dramatic? How's this? Yeah, I think that'll
work.

[*He opens the box.*]

A sweater. You know what this means? They probably got
me a PRIUS CONVERTIBLE!! I mean, it makes so much
sense! It's February, it's still cold out, and if I want to pop the
roof down, they don't want me to catch a cold. I mean, they
are my parents, right? They worry about those things. . . .

Bro, bro, bro, bro. They definitely make Prius convertibles.
They don't? How would you know—you're not a Toyota
salesman. Okay, maybe they really don't make them, but
what if my parents got one custom-made for me? I mean,
turning sixteen and getting your learner's permit is a big
deal. Like, I don't know if I'm ever going to do anything as
important again in my life!

Allan, I hope that someday you are as happy as I am right
now. But don't worry, maybe one day your parents will pass
on their old Prius to you. And if they don't, maybe I can give
you my Prius convertible, you know, if my parents let me. I
mean, by then I'll be eighteen, and they'll probably buy me a
different car. I'm definitely not buying you a sweater,
though—you'll have to buy your own.

Hey, bro! Bro, bro, bro, where you going? Aren't we gonna play *Super Smash Bros.*? Also, I need to practice my surprise face a few more times. Look! My surprise face is already feeling a little fake! If you don't come back, I'm never gonna give you my green Prius convertible! You'll just have to walk everywhere! You're gonna look pretty silly as an adult walking to the game store!

The Sensual Camper

Gina Nicewonger

CALVIN, 11 to 13

CALVIN *is a student on a middle-school camping trip. He is artistic, opinionated, and sassy; a huge fan of Miley Cyrus; and a connoisseur of grilled cheese. He is not athletic, but believes his passion for life places him heads above any other middle-school student. In fact, he would normally never seek out the company of his PE teacher, Coach Tanner, but the bad weather is keeping the whole school in close quarters, and a trip to the souvenir shop has given the two a rare opportunity to bond. Here,* CALVIN *is speaking to Coach Tanner, who is a chaperone on a class camping field trip. They are sitting together inside the camping lodge.*

CALVIN   Coach Tanner, guess what I got in the gift shop.

No. No one wants a sweatshirt to remind them of how our whole grade was trapped in this snowy hellhole with no heat for a week! Sorry if that was rude, but it's true and you know it, cuz you're freezing, too.

[*Beat.*]

So, guess what I got in the gift shop. Fine. A mood ring! And you want to know the craziest thing? It's right. My mood. The ring is detecting my mood accurately.

[*Beat.*]

Well, don't you want to know? What my mood is. You wanna guess? Okay! I'll tell you. Sensual. And, I AM sensual, Coach Tanner. Isn't that great?

Oh, get your head out of the gutter. Yes, I know what it means, and it's not what you think it means. "Sensual" just means "passionate." Passionate about senses and stuff. Like, Coach Tanner, how I love food and have been dreaming of an Asiago grilled-cheese sandwich and a tomato-basil soup to warm these old hands of mine. And you know I love music. God, I miss my Miley, while we waste away singing these stupid campfire songs. And art. Hello, I designed the class mural. Because I'm an artist. Because I'm sensual.

Maybe you don't understand because you're a jock. Jocks can't be sensual. And sensuals, like myself, can't be jocks.

Hey now. I know I said it, but you don't have to agree so passionately. Looks like Brian got a ring, too.

[*Shouting to Brian.*]

Brian, what color? What's your mood? Oh, really? You too?

[*To Coach.*]

Coach Tanner, between you and me, that surprises me.

[*Shouting to more guys.*]

Guys, you got rings? What's your mood? Yeah? Cool.

[*To Coach.*]

I can't believe it. I just can't believe it. I guess everyone's a sensual these days. Dang, my hands are cold! Wait a minute. What a rip-off.

[CALVIN *throws his ring off and yells in a dramatic fashion.*]

This ring isn't telling us our mood! It's telling us that we're cold! And we all know we're cold because we're can feel cold, dammit.

[CALVIN *realizes everyone is looking at him, and he quietly returns to the Coach.*]

Excuse me. That little fit was such a sensual thing to do.

DJ Ben Blake

Chris Quintos

BEN BLAKE, 16 to 18

BEN BLAKE *is an affable teenage host and aspiring entertainer.*
He considers himself a comedian. He takes his job, doing his high
school's morning announcements, very seriously. He's the kind of
guy who knows everyone's name.

BEN   Good morning St. Mary's High. I'm Ben Blake and
today is March 20th. We are on a block 2 schedule, a block 2
schedule. A friendly Ben-ly tip: Be sure to check out
Google's doodle if you haven't already—it's a good one
celebrating the equinox for all you pagans out there. And
here are today's announcements.

From the desk of our very own prin-ci-pal, Mrs. Knight, a
gentle reminder to all juniors and seniors with parking passes.
Parking in the faculty lot is not allowed and will result in
quality afterschool time in her office, aka detention. Yikes!

Just one more week for the Food Bank's Canned Goods
Drive! If you have extra cans lying around the house, or I

bet if you ask your mom really nicely, she'll put together a whole bag for you. Please don't forget to bring them in. Or better yet—walk across the street to Mario's corner store, say hello to good ole Mario, lay down a buck, and walk right back over here! The collection box is outside the upperclassmen student lounge.

Next, we have a few messages from Student Government. There have been multiple complaints about the line for the microwave in the cafeteria being too long. Our partisan pals over at StuGov would like to remind everyone that there is also a microwave available in the Student Government office. Stop on by, heat up your lunch, and heat up the debate on campus topics while you wait! I for one will be there to heat up my mac and cheese, and to "fire off" some questions about off-campus lunch privileges.

Spring Formal tickets are now available at StuGov's Social Window. A quick reminder, no one has asked this handsome guy out yet. So if you're looking for a roaring good time, stop by my locker in Building 4—I even own a tux! I'm kidding. Not really—I actually do own a tux, and am happy to coordinate with your beautiful dress. So, come find me between fourth and fifth period or sixth and seventh. Building 4, locker 413. Be there or be without a fabulous date, ladies!

The crew team is looking for a new cock-shin? I kid. A coxswain for the male team—men and women are welcome to apply. Here's to equal rights, folks! They have a regatta very early Saturday morning against Holy Name (booo!) and would like to see you there. Go Cats!

Mathlete tryouts are tomorrow. Please see Tom at his usual corner in the library for details. Sadly, I will be there— looking for a tutor as my math grades are wamp, wamp.

In brighter news, our cross-country team left Bishop High in the dust yesterday afternoon, taking them to finals next week. Rawr!

And that's all for today. As usual, I'm Ben Blake, and Enjoy the Equinox . . . Go Cats!

NRB

Brendan McCay

KYLE, 13 to 15

KYLE *is a bit frustrated with his body. He and his best friend, Skylar, are comparing bad days in Skylar's garage, and KYLE explains the devastating effects of puberty—and how they are ruining his life.*

KYLE Well that's not embarrassing at all, Skylar! Do you want to know what kind of HELL my body put me through this morning? No? Well I'm going to tell you anyway. You know how I've been in LOVE with Brittany Balsz for this entire school year, right? Well, Mrs. Jensen finally put me right behind her in English class about a week ago and it HAD been going great until today. So Mrs. J was passing back our grammar exams from last week and she was having each student come up and get their paper when their name was called. No big deal, right? WRONG. I was chatting it up with Brittany, we were flirting and making fun of Matt Tat again, when out of the blue I get this N.R.B. . . . Really Sky? You have so quickly forgotten what that delightful

acronym stands for? It means NO REASON BONER. Last
time I checked, there was nothing arousing about grammar
papers OR Matt Tat, so my conclusion is that this particular
boner was caused by nothingness—the soothing drone of
Mrs. Jensen just told my body, "It's GO TIME."

Do you see what kind of shorts I am wearing today Skylar?
Feel this material. That shit is thinner than board shorts for
goodness sakes! I would have killed for some thick denim
jeans or thick canvas cargo shorts, but no. I had to wear my
summertime boner pants. And to make matters worse, I
forgot my binder at home today too. So the old "boner
shield" option was out. ALSO I wasn't wearing a belt, so the
"tuck 'n' hide" method was also out of commission. Zero
boner-hiding tools at my disposal, Skylar—ZERO!

Anyway, I was making fun of this prank call I dropped on
Matt Tat last week when my name was called. At that
moment I lost all reason and brain function. I didn't try to
hide it, Sky. My hands didn't even reach to cover up. I stood
up and let my NRB flag fly. Brittany Balsz's eyes were
immediately fixated on my puberty-enraged stiffy and she
said, and I quote, "WHAT THE HELL?" She looked at me
like I had just punched a baby! I sat down immediately and
somehow a combination of embarrassment, nervousness,
and science reversed my NRB and it disappeared
instantaneously. I stood up quickly with my normal shaped
loins and asked Ms. Balsz in a nonchalant and annoyed

manner, "What?!" I pretended like it never happened. I got my paper and Brittany didn't turn back for the rest of the period. I don't know if she ever will again, Skylar.

So don't tell me that your body is doing weird stuff, because my penis just ruined my chances for true love today—all right?!

Your Mom Is a MILF

Alessandra Rizzotti

TODD, 15

TODD is totally unaware that he is a fantasy freak, and makes his friend uncomfortable when he talks about how hot his friend's mom is.

TODD   Hey dude, I didn't want to say this, but I gotta because it's like every time I come over, I just want to like kiss your mom or something. She's so hot. Like she's like, woah.

What? Shut up. You don't think the same thing. That's weird, dude. That's like Oedipussy or something. Like are you serious? My mind is blown, because my mom is like, ugly. I would never think she was MILFY.

What? Shut up. You think my mom's a MILF? No way. Her hair is like brown or something. Brown hair is NOT sexy. You gotta have red or blonde to get into my junk, ya know what I mean?

You're so regular, dude. It's like that time you thought Stacy was cute and she was like, NOT. I mean, woah . . . where are your priorities?

Hey dude, want to get drunk tonight? Just wondering. Because like I want to party, but I don't want to do it alone. Just want to be responsible.

Man, your mom is coming. Ah! She's so hot. I mean, I'm glad you agree, but I have first dibs when she divorces your dad. Just saying. I'll be a great second husband when I'm like thirty or something.

Oh dude, don't say you want to be my brother. That's gross. I can be your dad, but not your brother. Not if I'm going to marry your mom. Come on!

King of the Wait List

Amber Collins-Parnell

HENRY, 17

HENRY *is a real average guy.* He has just been waitlisted to *another college.* He has gone a bit crazy and is talking to himself *in his room.*

HENRY   Hear ye! Hear ye! King of the Wait List!

Friends, family—even you, my stupid hamster—that is what you must now call me! From here on out, King of the Wait List! Cheers to being half as good as the overachievers! Cheers to being better than the peasant, C average. All of you, bow down to my mediocre pizzazz . . . Royalty finally reaches the common man, the middle-class masses. Jackson would be proud. Anyhow, they don't love me, but they don't exactly hate me. I'd call it the toughest crowd. Wait-listed at all seven universities is quite an accomplishment. Not many can claim that.

I guess it isn't the worst possible situation, just more waiting, tense family dinners, and the usual evaluating my self-worth type of thing. I need to distinguish myself in some way. [*Beat.*] Hmmm, I wonder how hot the admissions officers are. Allison might not take it well, but this is Yale we are talking about. She'd have to understand. Her situation was different, of course. She's already in Harvard thanks to generations and generations of family alumni and hefty donations over the years. If only my parents invested in Apple stocks or something years back.

[*Beat.*]

Or, maybe I could write the admissions board? I demand to be accepted! Direct, forceful, clear. They'd know I'm not playing games here.

Well, no, maybe that's too aggressive. I need a tragedy, a sob story. A traumatic event that transformed my life, mentally and physically. Reality was too hard to accept . . . I turned to God. My atheist parents couldn't handle a theist. I was thrown out on the streets. Oh, I've got it! I died! [*Beat.*] Almost died! Jumped in front of an old lady who accidentally walked into oncoming traffic. Wait, too cliché. I got really sick. A few years back, I remember. A disease? Hey MOM! MOM?! [*Calling into the next room.*] What was that thing Grandpa got after the war? [*No response. Long pause.*] Gosh, I can't lie. I'll be audited, or something! My application was different. That fourth year of astronomy club and my alleged piano skills can slide. Someone has got to be checking the facts, though. Traumatic events may be too risky. And guilt? I'm not sure how my conscience would take it if it actually worked . . .

I'd like to get in on my own merit, my own ability. I don't want to have to pretend to stand out! I do! At least I think I do. I don't need Yale to tell me so. To hell with Yale! If the school doesn't want me, then I don't want it. Forget your King.

Hi, I'm Henry and I'm going to be okay.

And Your Name Is?

Chris Quintos

JACK, late teens

The shy, quiet JACK, *a barista, confesses details to his older sister about his crush on a customer named Carrie and the man he wishes he was.*

JACK   Carrie. Her name is Carrie. C-a-r-r-i-e. She comes in every day and she is . . . she's just really cute. I think I'm in love with her. Which is crazy, because I've never said more than five words to her. Mostly, "What can I get for you today?" And then calling her name when her drink is done. She works at the Forever 21 on Market Street.

I don't know how people do it. I have this coworker, Tim— he just flirts with everyone. I dunno, he's like twenty-one or twenty-two or something, so he's a little older than me. But like—he's got mad game. You know? Like, I feel like Beyoncé could walk in here tomorrow, and Tim would get her laughing in thirty seconds. It's like watching a magician. Like, where does he come up with this stuff, you know? It's hard enough for me to ask what people want to drink. And I'm supposed to do that. And then calling out names—that part is hard, too. I guess because I'm kind of quiet. Except for Carrie—if I'm working the register, I don't even ask. "Tall Iced Chai with Soy for Carrie." I don't know. Like sometimes, I'll be floating around in my mind while I'm making drinks, then when I have to call out a name, I do it quietly. And then I know it's like—I HAVE to do it again. But I'm like—ugh—why didn't I say it loudly to begin with? If I just said it with a little confidence, I wouldn't have to repeat myself.

Tim never repeats himself. Well, unless maybe the customer isn't paying attention. And then he'll add a joke, like, "Slightly less warm unclaimed Americano for Tom." God, Tim is so cool. Like, why am I so timid. Like I know this Half-Caff Latte is for Matt—I've made it for him for like four months, most mornings. So, why can't I just say that: "Half-Caff Latte for Matt. Half-Caff Latte for Matt." Twice, with confidence. And like, Matt—that's like a normal name. Don't even get me started on the hard names. Like—are *q*'s supposed to sound like *c*'s or *k*'s? So hard to keep track. And like—apparently there's more than one way to say and spell every name you thought you knew. Like, not "Matt"— because "Matt" is pretty self-explanatory—but like "Sonia." Some people are like super specific, like it's "So-ni-ah" or like "Son-ya."

I don't know. Or like if I spell something with a *y* instead of an *ie*, that like could ruin someone's day. You know? It could end up on their Instagram as an FML. And I don't want that.

I make sure to spell Carrie's name right every time. I get upset when other people don't. Sometimes they spell it, K-e-r-r-y or C-a-r-e-y. But like, Tim? He could spell her name with a *Z* and she'd still laugh at his jokes. I just know she would.

Allowance Negotiations

Jessica Glassberg

MIKE, 15

MIKE, *carrying a plate of sandwiches, enters the family room in his house and feigns surprise to find his parents sitting on the couch.*

MIKE   Oh hey, Mom and Dad. I was in the kitchen, grabbing myself a snack thinking, "I bet Mom and Dad want a bite, too." So, help yourselves.

[*Pointing around the platter.*]

There's some PB and J over there and some turkey and swiss on the end.

[*After a moment:*]

And sure, Mom made these, but knowing the selfless woman you are, you'd just let us all enjoy. Well, Mom, it's time for you to enjoy. You, too, Dad; get in there.

[*Looking at his watch.*]

Well, I have to finish up my econ paper . . . gotta keep that straight-A streak going. Plus, I'm taking take Rachel on a date tomorrow, and I've got some planning to do. Enjoy your snacks. You know where to find me.

[MIKE *goes to leave and as he is about to exit, he turns back.*]

Ya know . . . Rachel's a pretty special girl. I want to treat her right. Ya know? Of course you know.

[MIKE *walks back up to his parents and sits down next to them.*]

But I'm just thinking about my current financial situation, and well, I don't really have a financial situation to tell ya the truth. So, I just wanted to see what you thought about my allowance . . . See, it hasn't gone up since the third grade. And I'm much better at emptying the dishwasher. I hardly ever break a glass and I don't lick the silverware anymore.

Yes, you provide a beautiful roof over my head, clothes on my back, and three meals a day. But what about those days I sleep through breakfast? Or I eat at a friend's house. That's essentially free money in your pocket. If you add all of that up, that's at least ten more dollars a week that could be headed in my direction so I can take a classy girl like Rachel out on the town.

[*Thinking, then:*]

I just . . . I look at the two of you and I think, wow. What a
special relationship. There's just so much I can learn from
you. Dad, I remember you told me that you took mom
ice-skating on your first date. You talked and snuggled up
together and helped each other around the rink. Hot
chocolate. Just perfect. You're such a smart guy. But, it
wasn't free, right? I mean, you didn't just find a frozen lake
and make the skates with your two hands. You had to put
some money into the date. And I know that I'm going to
have to do that with Rachel. Not that she's expecting
something extravagant. She's not into material things. She
reminds me a lot of you, Mom. She's a good girl. But isn't
that the kind of girl you want to spend money on? Get
things for?

[*Not getting anywhere, defeated:*]

Okay. I'm a nerd. I get straight As and I adore my parents.
No girl could really like me, right? Rachel's doing this out of
pity. I'll go back to my room, finish my paper, and call
Rachel to cancel the date.

[MIKE *gets up to leave again.*]

Is this what you want? You want a quitter? You want me to
just quit? I have the chance to go on a date. A real date.
With a sweet girl. I'm not going to use the money on booze
or drugs. I'm not going to knock her up. I don't even know
if I'm going to kiss her.

[*Then, angry:*]

Do you know how many teenagers don't even talk to their parents?!? Do you know how many teenagers are flunking out of school and aren't in the French Honors Society and don't volunteer at the food bank? And all I'm asking for is a few extra bucks each week.

[MIKE*'s dad gives him a twenty.*]

Thank . . . thank you. You won't regret increasing my allowance. This is a real game changer. You're the best. The absolute best!

[MIKE *leaves and after a beat, pops his head back in.*]

Oh, since I'll be going on that date with Rachel tomorrow, I won't have time to clean the bathroom or do the laundry. So, thanks for understanding. You really are the best!

My Mom Thinks I'm a Pervert

Kate McKinney

JORDAN, 16

JORDAN *is sitting in a chair in a psychiatrist's office, facing the doctor.*

JORDAN   I guess you know why I am here, Dr. Sawyer. My mom thinks I'm a total pervert, and she thinks I am lying to her when I tell her I'm not!

I guess for your average teenage boy, that would be an accurate description but . . . for me, it's just not true at all. I'm a pretty decent kid. My grades are fine, I keep my room pretty tidy. But my mom assumes that under my mild-mannered facade, I'm Hugh Hefner padding through the halls of Mountain View High School in slippers and a satin smoking jacket, while three women in bikinis let me beat them at *Missile Command*. That's not a euphemism by the way. Hugh Hefner irrationally loves old Atari games. I'm not kidding— look it up sometime. And that almost tells you all you need to know about me right off the bat: I'm sixteen years old, straight as an arrow, but I know more about the video-gaming habits of Hugh Hefner than I do about the female anatomy.

I'm not sure why she thinks that, except that she's friends with a bunch of other moms of teenage boys and they are all hormone-engorged cavemen so she assumes it's true for me, too. I kind of wish I was like that! It would be easier. I'm like Steve Carrel in *The 40-Year-Old Virgin*, pretending I know what a woman's breast feels like, only in my case I'm pretending to know what a woman's breast LOOKS like.

Okay, I know what they look like but not because I sought out the information! I've read *National Geographic* and stumbled across rain-soaked *Playboys* while out on my bike! But I've never deliberately looked at a naked woman. I mean, don't get me wrong. I like girls. I have . . . feelings. But trying to make them happen just feels creepy to me.

I know I'm not "normal"! And maybe that's the deal with my mom. She wants me to be normal. And it's normal for teenage boys to be sex crazed. Sometimes she tries to test me. I think one of my siblings got into her birth control stash, because once she confronted me with an empty plastic wrapper. "Do you know what was in this?" she demanded in that voice where's she's barely on the edge of reason, which is most of the time. "A lollipop?" I said, completely serious. She stalked off angrily, and I realized it was a CONDOM wrapper. And she just thought I was being a smart-ass.

And then, of course, there's the day she accused me of watching a dirty movie. The library left a message on the answering machine (yes, my parents have an ANSWERING MACHINE) to let me know my copy of *Welcome to the Dollhouse* was overdue. My mom could barely even look at me while she relayed the message, then added (with teeth clenched), "I didn't know the library stocked PORNOGRAPHY." "Mom . . . it's an independent film by Todd Solondz." "Watching filth isn't the way to independence! You're grounded!"

After that, she hid all of her old workout tapes and starting throwing away every catalog with a bra section. And when my chemistry partner Kendra came over to work on a project, she kept making up excuses to come in and catch us in the "act." The act of memorizing the periodic table, I guess. Don't worry, Mom, we don't actually have any "chemistry."

It would almost be easier if I was what she thought—a mouth-breather with a perpetual boner. But I feel like she's wasting all this effort. I'm exactly the kind of boy she wants and she doesn't even realize it. I'm not getting anyone pregnant. I'm barely even thinking about it. But I guess there's no chance of it happening if my mom continues to act as a human shield whenever we walk past Victoria's Secret. Even if I change, I'm sure she won't. I'm just done with arguing about it! Maybe you could talk to her—I figure if she hears it from a man with a diploma, then maybe she'll lay off!

Do the Stupid Homework

Cooper McHatton

ALBERT BENSON, 17

ALBERT *sits at a desk, talking to another student through video chat on his laptop. Homework litters the table, a bunch of textbooks are open, and a few empty cups are scattered around.*

ALBERT   You know that scene in *The Iron Giant* where he's all hyped up on espresso and explaining how frustrating he finds other students? I can TOTALLY relate.

He rants, "I JUST DO THE STUPID HOMEWORK!" and seriously, why is that so hard? I'm always getting [*Whiny.*] ". . . you're so smart." [*Whiny.*] ". . . you're a genius." But, the truth be told . . . I'm not.

You want people to call you smart too? 'Cause I have the secret. Got a pen handy? It's gonna change your life.

Ready?
JUST DO THE HOMEWORK!

You want an A in the class? Go to class, take notes, and finish all of your homework between classes. Does that seem much too impossible? Does it seem . . . out of reach?

I saw you last night online at 3:00 a.m. I was studying. You were posting GIFs. When I was going through flashcards outside of class, you were texting. I got an A, you got a C . . . and you were HAPPY WITH THAT! I cringe at an A minus! Why bother going at all?

What do you mean, it's because you're not good at this subject and so a C is pretty good?

I can't believe you're saying it again! NO! I am not smarter than you. I just study! Geez, what am I not getting here?

What?

You're mad about that?

Everyone is mad about that?

But he forgot to assign the homework. I HAD to remind him.
But then we'd be behind.

Oh that, too?! Well . . . he said there was going to be a pop quiz and he forgot.
If you're not going to class to get the most out of it, stay home.

. . . Oh, that's why you stayed home?

No, I didn't go to that party.

[*Longingly.*] SHE was THERE?

[*Adamantly.*] Doesn't she know there is going to be a QUIZ tomorrow?

Job Applicant

Carla Cackowski

THOMAS, 16

THOMAS, *a high school student, is interviewing for his first job. The interviewer sits down across from him.*

THOMAS   Yes, that is correct. I have a 4.0 GPA, sir, yes. Well, my parents thought it would be a good idea for me to expand my horizons this summer by obtaining employment. I mean, *we! We* thought it would be a good idea for me to expand my horizons. Well, sir, they feel—I mean, I! *We! We* feel that a part-time job would be good for me as I transition into my junior year of high school. Honestly, my parents— and I!—*we* would have loved for me to have gotten a job when I was in middle school, but the child labor laws are difficult to ignore, especially when your next-door neighbor is a city-elected judge. He asks a lot of questions and my parents say we have to stay on his good side so he will write me a letter of recommendation when I apply to Stanford next year.

Oh no, sir. I do not need the money from this job for college. My parents and I—we!—are very confident I will receive scholarships from multiple universities that will cover any financial obligation I may take on as a college student. They—we—discussed it thoroughly, sir, and decided that having a job to list on my college applications is just another skill I can add to my already long list of accomplishments. Also, currently, I have no friends. My mother would like me to make some. She thinks it would be helpful so that I may include "social skills" on my college applications. Do you happen to employ other teenage boys currently looking for friends? Unsure? How about teenage girls?

No, sir. No need to worry. I will not be distracted by girls while on the job. I currently have no girlfriend. Actually, I've never had a girlfriend and have no plans on getting one any time soon. Unless you know of one in need of a boyfr— nevermind. My parents don't want me to date. Nor do I! My parents and I, both of us, together, we, neither of us want me to date right now. You can't list "good at dating" on a college application, now can you . . . Can you? If you find out you can, will you let me know and I will tell my parents and then maybe they'll change their minds?

Qualities I can bring to this position? Well, sir, I'm very intelligent. I have a strong ability to assess a situation as it arises and quickly react with confidence. My communication skills are top-notch, as I am the state champion in speech and debate. I am able to control the modulation of my voice with such effectiveness that I can persuade just about anyone to do whatever I need them to do. [*In a deep voice:*] I need for you to give me this job. [*Normal voice:*] Did it work? Not yet? Not a problem! My greatest skill is that I never give up in the face of adversity!

I'm hired? Really? Thank you so much, sir! I will not let you down! [*Relieved, to self:*] Maybe now my parents will finally get off my back. [*Self-conscious, to interviewer:*] I mean, I! We! Maybe we will finally get off my back.

Um, sir. One quick thing before you ask for my bathing suit size. I don't swim. Yes, I know this is a job interview for a lifeguard. . . . But I achieved high scores on both my written and paramedic tests! Well, sir, forgive my tone, but it's not my fault you didn't ask to see my swim test scores before bringing me into your office. Of course, the ability to actually swim is important, but I feel that with persistence I can be an excellent swimmer . . . one day. Just not today. But probably in a couple of weeks. A week? How about a couple of days? What if I promise to come to work tomorrow having learned to swim? Sir, please don't leave, I really need this job, my parents really need for me to need this job, and I need whatever my parents need of me so I will be a successful adult who may not ever have a real emotional experience, but will always pay my bills on time and rise to a level of success that my peers will envy and my parents will rejoice in!

[*On knees.*] Please, sir, please! I really need to get out of my parents house for a few hours a week!

[*He composes himself.*]

Sure, I can hand out towels. I'll be an excellent towel-hander-out person. Thank you, sir. Thank you.

Going to the Chapel

Kathy S Yamamoto

THAD, 13

THAD is a romantic, mature thirteen-year-old who is looking for the perfect girl in all the wrong places. Here, THAD is at a wedding, congratulating the new groom.

THAD   Hey dude. Congratulations. Getting married is a huge deal.

Can I tell you a secret? I hate weddings. I know you probably don't want to hear this because it's your wedding, blah, blah blah, but now that you've married my cousin, we're family, and I can be honest.

I hate weddings. And I've been to a lot of weddings, this spring alone! Do you know how hard it is, to be a thirteen-year-old at a wedding? SO hard. You're surrounded by beautiful women—and I'm not talking about the flower girls—I'm talking model-aged women. They're all shiny from dancing, and are smiling all the time in case someone takes a picture.

In a word, they're perfect.

And there are so many of them! They're in the photo booth with ironic mustaches, they're in the bathroom putting on lipstick, they're at the candy bar sneaking in more gummy sharks when their friends aren't looking, and they're all over that dance floor.

Now, I know that when people think of attractive women dancing, they think of people in a club. Short skirts, grinding up against one another. I've never been to a club, but I watch MTV all the time at night after my parents go to bed so I know. This isn't that sort of dancing. But it's still beautiful to watch.

Yeah, you might think I'm romantic, but it's true. This is a breeding ground for future wives. And they're thinking it, too—I mean who wouldn't after a three-hour-long ceremony? "Do you take her . . ." I mean you just have to start imagining yourself in that position!

But it doesn't matter. Because when you're thirteen, it doesn't matter how many potential wives there are in the room—they ignore you. Or worse, they'll laugh at you.

I asked Shannon Daughtry to dance and she giggled! After that, my dance with her was ruined. The romance in the air dissipated. And we were dancing to Josh Groban. He can make any mood romantic, even one between my parents.

And I'm not bad looking, either. I'm like a young Frank Sinatra, you know, before the drug and alcohol abuse. When everything was still bright and sunny. I got good skin, a sense of humor, and a mature outlook . . . that's what my nanna tells me anyway. Then why can't I find a girl who'll marry me?

I figure if I can't find a woman to marry, I could always drown myself in work. That's what Uncle Mark does. He's a banker. But I couldn't do that. Math isn't my favorite subject. And not just because Mr. Clayton, he's my math teacher, not just because he always gives higher grades to girls. I think I'd have to stick to something I know. Probably an MTV VJ or something like that. I could introduce videos and artists. Also, if I forget a name of the song or the singer it wouldn't matter, because it's late at night and only thirteen-year-old kids who don't have wives would be watching.

I'm so happy for you though, dude. You got it all made.

No, I know, that's what everyone says. I'll find the right girl eventually. Bruno Mars has said it. Jay Z has said it. Hell, even Nicki Minaj has said it. But I don't know if that's true. If I can't find a single girl who will take me seriously here, where there are so many eligible women, then where?

See—watch this.

[*To a woman to his right.*]

Hi Illyssa, you're looking really nice in that peach dress. Would you maybe like to dance with me? I talked to the DJ, and Josh Groban will be playing soon?

See? Sure she said she'd dance with me, but she was laughing the whole time! As if I'm some sort of joke!

I guess I'll just have to be an MTV VJ. I hope they'll admit me into the club.

Hershey Pants

Kathy S Yamamoto

LOREN, 13

LOREN is the smartest kid in class. You know the type—always wears a button-up shirt and tie to school, skipped a grade early on, and is incredibly intelligent. The only difference with LOREN is that he genuinely believes people are good. Here, he finally gains the courage to confront his bullies.

LOREN Hey Mark, Antonio, DeShawn. You've spent the last semester bullying me, making me feel badly for how well I do in school, stealing my rollie-backpack and putting it on top of the flagpole . . . You guys even single-handedly ruined my presidential campaign this year—and probably forever—by telling our entire school that I was a pedophile. I'm only thirteen! I'm technically a minor! How could I be a pedophile!?

You've all been so horrible to me, and I would often sit up at night, unable to get my recommended eight and a half hours of sleep, wondering why. Why would a person, unprovoked,

be so cruel to another? What could I have possibly done to
you to inspire such malice? Just in case anyone is confused,
"malice" means "evil." I don't mean to be pretentious, but I
know for a fact that none of you have kept up with the
literature reading.

I know most bullied people take solace in knowing that one
day in the future, they will be very rich, while the ones who
bully them will all be very poor, or likely in jail, but with this
economy, who knows if that'll be true. And besides, my real
passion right now is prison reform, meaning hopefully jail
won't be such a bad place for you guys if you get there.

I was thinking about it, though, and I realized, you guys
spend a lot of time on me. Deductively speaking, you spend
more time thinking of what pranks to pull on me, executing
those pranks, improvising terrible interactions with me,
talking to other people about me, probably more than you
do about any other person. That made me feel really good. I
mean, it seems clear to me that the only reason you are all
paying so much attention to me is because you want to be
my friend. To which my response is, of course!

Obviously, it'll be awkward in the beginning. After all, you
guys were so cruel! But my father was in a fraternity in his
youth, Phi Beta Kappa, in which the initiation required
much humiliation and tomfoolery. But despite that, my dad
has remained good friends with all of his fraternity brothers,
and talks of those hazing days with nostalgia. I know in

twenty-five years, when I'm visiting you all in jail, talking about the ways we can remake the American prison system into a place for reform rather than a place where corporations profit, we can look back on the day you put a Hershey's bar on my seat so everyone thought I defecated myself. That was a good one, guys. I had to throw away those khakis! No worries, though—they still had them in stock at Costco, and I bought two pairs, just in case.

And look, I get it. Why you're so desperate for a new friend. I mean, three's a tough number for a group, someone's always being left out, am I right, Mark? Plus, I bring some obvious advantages to this dynamic—my high level of computing and overall intelligence makes the average intelligence of the group 2.35 times higher, I have an impressive DVD collection which includes the Pixar Shorts, every single Miyazaki film—even the obscure ones—and obviously Sherlock. My extensive list of allergies makes eating out harder, but I usually can find something at all those chain restaurants you guys seem to like so much.

I guess what I'm trying to say is, I figured it out. I would love to be your friend, mostly because I lack daily human interaction with my peer group and I'm tired of eating lunch in Mrs. Brister's room—it kind of smells of day-old sushi. Also, in the future, if you ever want to be friends with me, or anyone else, again, might I suggest just asking them to be your friend, or if that's too straightforward, asking them to hang out with you? It seems to me that we wasted a lot of time on pranks when we could've been hanging out, you know, being normal kids and disassembling a computer or something. I'm just happy we can now be the best friends we were meant to be.

Oh, are we off on our first friend adventure? This should be fun. You're taking me in the direction of the girls' restroom. Not what I might imagine where male friends might congregate, but hey, I'm new to the group, and I'll follow your lead.

[*He touches the seat of his pants.*]

Oh no! Hershey bar again!? I hope Costco will still be open when my parents get home.

First Date

Rachel Raines

DEREK, 17 to 19

DEREK *is sitting in a small, quiet Chinese restaurant, during an afternoon lunch date.*

DEREK   Hey! I mean, hello, hi, how are you? Wow, ha-ha, that was four greetings, wasn't it? Welp, I guess I've covered that territory for the night . . . let's talk about the weather next!!

Ha-ha, no I'm clearly kidding. Because that's boring and first dates are fun! So yeah, I was just joking, are you okay? Is this table fine? We could move if the air vent is bothering you; it's making a humming sound, you hear that? It's like MMMMMMMMMMMMMMMMMMMMMMMM—you hear it? MMMMMMMMMMMMM . . . what? Oh, yeah, sorry I can stop making that sound.

So what do you do for a living? A nurse? Yeah, I knew that because it said so on your profile. Have you gotten many matches from that yet? Oh well, I've had about, eh, fifteen?

They don't tend to work out for me, ha-ha; I'm hoping
you're lucky number sixteen! You know, like a racehorse?
Not that you have a horse face! I mean your face is long and
you do have long hair, and it's black like horsehair . . . but,
you don't look like a pony or anything, ha-ha. So yeah, I'm a
tour guide at the art museum in the park.

So do you like this restaurant? I thought since you're
Chinese you would like a Chinese restaurant. I mean you
could like other food, too; we could get Italian on our next
date . . . Oh! Um, I'm sorry—I didn't realize you were
Korean.

So . . . the dumplings are good. Here, have another! I say eat
as much as you want. Men shouldn't judge your body! And
they wouldn't anyway, you have a nice body! Not that I only
looked at you body, I just noticed you have a nice "female"
shape, ha-ha, so good job doing that, ha-ha. I mean,
assuming everything is real of course. I mean, it all looks
real! I haven't felt any of it yet, ha-ha, so I don't *know* it's real
but it looks great! Tip-top shape!

So yeah, I was thinking after this we could maybe drive back
to my place, and by my place, I mean my parents . . . because
I've got a bottle of wine chilling in the fridge. You ordered
red but white is better for you so you should drink that
anyway, or we could stop and get a bottle of red. Obviously,
I have a fake id . . . oh, you have plans for later? Okay, well I
would love to take you home and walk you to your door, I'm

sure you have a nice house and I would love to find out
where you live 'cause I need to know if it'll be a difficult
commute from my place anyway, you know? I really want to
make sure we have a solid foundation for a future, I really
am feeling a connection here, I mean I meet a girl online
and she turns out to be professional, beautiful, and smart?!
We really hit the jackpot didn't we? . . . Sorry, what was your
name again?

Pillow Talk

Leah Mann

DANNY, 15

DANNY, *an awkward teen, sits with his girlfriend on top of his bed. The blankets are rumpled. He is flustered and sincere.*

DANNY Whoo! Wow. That was . . . yup. I get it, all the hype and everything. Thank you. Like super duper oh my god where do I even start—THANK YOU. You're . . . So nice. Like, the nicest, and I know a lot of nice people. I mean my crowd in general is, like, the nice guys but you . . . you're like the princess of niceness and kindness. But you're more than that, because you're smart, too, and really pretty. You know that, how pretty you are? You hair is like super soft and your lips are so pink. Maybe that's lip gloss, because they taste like raspberries.

[*Beat.*]

I didn't think you'd even want to talk to me. When I asked you out, it was a dare. Not like a bet in a bad way, but because I was too chickenshit and Dougie knew the only way

I'd ever have the balls to talk to you like that was if he dared me. I can't say no to a dare—it's a weakness of mine I guess.

[*Beat.*]

But I beat him! I did it first. He's only gotten to second base. I'm not totally clear on what counts as second base, but we definitely beat that.

[*Beat.*]

Not that it's a contest. Just being here with you makes me a winner. It felt different than I thought it would. Better. The human body is awesome, isn't it? You learn stuff in bio and health class and whatever, but to see it and feel it firsthand!

[*Beat.*]

Maybe I'll be a doctor. Wouldn't my mom love that? What do you want to be when you grow up? Not to be lame, but think about it—isn't it a funny question? I mean, when do you count as grown-up? It is like the day you leave for college or the day you start your first job or when you have a kid?

[*Beat.*]

I'm sorry I'm talking so much—it's your eyes. They make me feel naked, like you can see everything I'm thinking. Like your eyes are binoculars into my soul and you can read all my secrets. So . . .

[*Beat.*]

So okay, I have to say something and I don't want you to freak out. Man, you're a great listener. Okay.

Here goes.

[*Beat.*]

I love you. I totally love you and it's not just because of what we did. I'm not saying it just to make you feel better or because I think I'm supposed to.

[*Beat.*]

Yeah, sure, I'm all tingly inside and out . . . Yes, our bodies merged into one and I've never felt so close to another human being in my entire life, but I loved you before.

[*Beat.*]

I loved you in class when you read the story you wrote and you were shaking because you were so nervous but your story was amazing! It was totally the best in the class and you're so talented but you don't know it. I loved you at field day when you had to run the three-legged race with Olivia who's the slowest kid in school and you didn't complain at all. I loved you at the fall dance when you were standing against the wall with your friends, chewing on your hair in that green dress. I loved you when you shared your French fries with me at lunch after I spilled soda on mine. I love you and it's okay if you don't love me back or don't want to say it, because I know it's a weird thing and we're young and I'm not saying it's forever or I want to get married.

[*Beat.*]

I'd rather you were my third wife so we could grow old and die together than my first marriage that doesn't work out and ends in a mean divorce where we don't even talk to each other. I'd never waste a shitty first marriage on you.

[*Beat.*]

I don't even care that you're going to homecoming with Chaz, because we shared something special, even if you share it with Chaz after the dance. Not that I'm calling you slutty. You're not, you're way classy and allowed to make your own decisions, which I completely respect.

[*Beat.*]

Wait . . . what do you mean that was only third base? It felt grand-slammy to me . . . are you sure? Hey, you're the expert.

[*Sighs.*]

I still love you, even from third base.

It's Me or You!

Jessica Glassberg

JASON, 14

JASON *is in his bedroom. From the audience's perspective, he is looking intently at, and speaking angrily to, someone—but we don't know who.*

NOTE: JASON *is actually looking into a mirror, but we don't want to reveal that yet. It should be kept vague.*

JASON I can't believe you showed up here today. Today! Today, the day I'm asking Melissa Carmichael to the eighth-grade dance! Well . . . it was going to be today. I can't exactly go up to her now that you're here.

[*Disappointed.*]

I spent all week thinking of just what to say.

[*Cooly, as if speaking to Melissa, 14.*]

Hey, Melissa . . . ya got a date for the dance?

[*After a deep, relieved breath.*]

It was perfect. And then she'd say no and I'd ask her to go with me and she'd say yes.

[*Remembering.*]

Well, I'm pretty sure she'd say yes. In English yesterday, when Mrs. Stewart was assigning parts for *A Midsummer Night's Dream*, she said, "Melissa Carmichael, you'll be Titania, and Oberon will be . . . Jason Weiss." And that was when Melissa turned and looked back to my desk. I expected an "ugh," or an "oh, man," or just a disappointed sigh. But she looked at me and smiled. I don't even know if I smiled back. I froze. Time froze. That's the first time I made a girl smile. Sure, my mom smiles at me all the time. That woman is obsessed with me. But I made Melissa smile and I knew that she would be the girl I'd go to the eighth-grade dance with. We'd joke with our kids someday about how it all started with us being a Shakespearean king and queen and then we went to the eighth-grade dance, and then prom, and then . . . everything.

[*Reality setting in.*]

But now, I can't ask her. Not today. Because of you.

[*Frustrated.*]

Today was the day. It's a Friday. It's perfect. When she said yes and I saw her at the mall on Saturday, we'd have a perfect conversation starter.

[*Then, almost in tears.*]

But I can't face her like this. With you. I'll get laughed at before I even open my mouth.

[*Thinking.*]

What if I don't ask her today and Brian Dorf asks her? She'd totally say yes to Brian Dorf. The guy plays like every sport and he shaves . . . his actual mustache. I have to get to her before Brian does.

[*Very serious.*]

Okay. That's it. It's you or me pal. You're a blemish on society and I'm not going down without a fight. It's time for Jason Weiss to man up. You wanted to squeeze me outta this. I'm gonna squeeze you out.

[JASON *aggressively tries and fails to pop a pimple on his face. He GRUNTS and CRINGES until he finally gives up.*]

[*Defeated.*]

You win . . .

[*Trying to regain confidence.*]

I can't face anyone like this. But come Monday morning, I'm going to show Melissa the kind of man I am!

[*Calling offstage, whining.*]

Mommy, I don't feel well.

Seventeen or Older

Mark Alderson

SHAWN, 14

SHAWN *and Brian, two young and clean-cut friends, are standing inside of a movie theater hallway, with a ticket in each of their hands.*

SHAWN Okay Brian, now is our chance. We can sneak into *Bloody Axe of Hell 4* without anyone looking. We've got the perfect plan for this situation. We've purchased *Happy Penguins 3D* tickets and unbeknownst to the theater manager, we will be finding ourselves a seat in this year's bloodiest movie.

I know it's sort of a lame plan, but that's the best I can do. We are only fourteen and even though we at look at *least* twenty-six, I still wasn't able to convince the ticket counter otherwise.

Look, if we get caught, just act supercool. Last time we got caught in the act, you vomited and they saw that as a sign of weakness. Let's keep this mission clean. The only bodily fluids I want to witness are on the big screen while we slurp down our slushies. By the way, thanks for buying my drink. I owe you one.

Look look! There is no one guarding the door. We can casually waltz in and grab our seats. It's only two minutes until the movie starts, so we will have to wait it out until it gets dark in the theater.

Are you ready, Brian? This could be the first crime we commit. If we get caught we are looking at like, two months in jail *at least*. So hombre, you wanna see this flick?

I know it's a scary movie. That's why they make them! Don't worry, if anything happens that you can't handle, I won't make fun of you if you close your eyes. Just don't make fun of me if I do the same.

This is it, Brian—our first R-rated movie adventure. We better hurry so we don't have to find a seat in the dark. That's such an amateur move.

Okay Brian, now is our chance. I hope *Bloody Axe of Hell 4* is as good as the critics say. And don't worry. I'm scared, too.

Crap! They spotted us. We better watch *Happy Penguins 3D* just to make sure they don't arrest us.

Good thing I actually wanted to see that . . .

[*The two friends rush into the theater with no one in sight.*]

YouTube Star

Alessandra Rizzotti

BRENDAN, 14

BRENDAN *is OCD on the Internet and has decided that his career is going to revolve around becoming Internet famous. He's hyperactive and has Asperger's, but he's naive and hopeful that his mom will let him follow his dreams.*

BRENDAN   I don't want to break it to you, but I do, because it's way big news that I'm the newest YouTube STAR. I'm not lying, Mom. I swear I don't have to go to college now. I have it all worked out. They gave me a contract and I'm going to make like $100 a week. I'm set!

Wanna see my characters? One is like this guy who is kinda lame and all he does is live at home and talk to people on the Internet and film videos of himself. Here goes: "Hey guys, I'm such a loser. I only ate brownies today and pet my cat! Ahhh! Isn't that NUTS!?!? Wacky dacky doodle do! Boop boop booop booop." And then I put sound effects and stuff and it's really cool because people like seeing special effects and I can do that, Mom. Like I didn't even have to go to film school to learn what I know. You'll be totally saving on college.

Only thing is, can I live with you the next few years so I can save up money for like getting new equipment and then maybe move out later? Just thinking about my future and the practicalities, because rent is like a million dollars these days.

I was thinking I could be like a YouTube star, and then on the side, act in commercials and design websites and stuff. That would be my way of making EXTRA cash. YouTube is where it's at! We should get a pet like a weird-looking cat and then the cat can be famous too. Or maybe a goldfish. Cats and dogs are too popular.

Anyways, I should probably get going. Think about me living here for the next seven years or so, doing YouTube videos for companies like Nike and Sam Ash. Probably you should invest in a green screen for me. Just saying. This house could be a multimillion-dollar studio—or just a boring place to live. You decide, Ma.

Outfield

Derek Heeren

KEVIN, 16

KEVIN *stands in right field. He is playing in his first varsity game, after the starting right fielder left the game because of an ACL injury.*

KEVIN   Okay, runners on second and third. One out. If it comes to you, throw to the cutoff. [*Mumbling—as a mantra:*] If it comes to you, throw to the cutoff. Second and third. Throw to the cutoff. Throw to the cutoff. DON'T overthrow him. Please, don't overthrow him again. God, you are the worst. [KEVIN *seizes to attention.*] PITCH! [*Relaxes.*] Strike.

Okay. Okay, okay, okay. Stop thinking about that. No balls, one strike, one out. Runners on second and third. Focus, Kevin, focus. Don't think about that throw. Don't think about giving up the lead. It's all right. Don't think about Holly seeing you cry. [*Sigh.*] I cannot believe you did that. It's okay. It's okay. Maybe you looked directly into the sun.

She doesn't know—you were blinded and teared up. That's your body's natural protection. You can't help that. What does she expect, that you have sunproof eyes? [*Snaps to attention again.*] PITCH! HIT!!! [*Relaxes.*] Foul . . .

It actually makes more sense that you were blinded than what actually happened. I'm sure that's what she guessed—she's very understanding. Like she's even here, Kevin. You're pathetic. [*Tenses.*] PITCH! HIT!!! [*Relaxes.*] Foul . . .

STOP IT! Focus! One out. Runners on second . . .heh, the guy on second looks like . . . oh, I can't think of his name. He was in those movies. With the vampires. Or the wizards. Was it Robert something? No. No. Um. Robert. No, you just said Robert. Uh. Ruh . . . Ruh . . . "R" name. Rob . . . Oh wait—was it . . . Robert? No! Stop saying Robert; It was not Robert!! PITCH! Ball.

Holly probably *is* here. To see her stupid pitcher boyfriend, "Weston." What kind of name is that for a person? That's a direction and a preposition. Oh God, I don't know what the count is. There's two outs, right? Or was it one? Should I ask someone? I've never seen an outfielder ask how many outs there are in the middle of an inning. If Holly is out there, she'll see you look like more of an idiot than you already did. Is she here? I can't see—it's so bright. PITCH! HIT!!! Oh God, I can't see it. Oh God, I can't see it! [*Cowering, swatting at the air with his glove.*] Oh God!!! [*Relaxes.*] Foul.

It's so bright out. Why didn't you bring sunglasses? Is the sun closer to the Earth today? Is that possible? That would really support that whole being-blinded thing. It does seem unusually warm. Come on, Kevin. Get your head in the game. Pitch! Hit! It's coming to me. IT'S COMING TO ME! This is it—this is going to turn things around. You're going to be a hero, Kevin. Holly is here and she's here to see you at THIS MOMENT! This moment where your baseball career and love life both take off! DON'T BLOW IT, DO YOU HEAR ME?! DO NOT BLOW IT!!!!!

[KEVIN *catches the ball.*]

[*Disbelieving.*] I got it . . . I got it! We win the game! You did it, Kevin! You did it! Everyone is cheering. [*Waving.*] You're welcome, everyone! They're all cheering and yelling and waving their arms and . . . wait. How many outs was it again? . . . Uh-oh.

Citizen's Arrest

Brandon Econ

JEFF-MICHAEL WALTERS III, 14

JEFF-MICHAEL's neighbor Tom Phillips is standing out on the curb by the trash cans when JEFF-MICHAEL, *who is sick and tired of Tom's nonsense, comes running out in his Star Wars pajamas to give his older neighbor a piece of his mind.*

JEFF-MICHAEL   Tom? Is it all right if I call you "Tom"? Well, have it your way, Mr. Phillips. I'm putting you under citizen's arrest.

What do you mean, why? Because you threw my bicycle in the tree. And then you said, "Let me get that down for you" and threw my helmet in the tree, too.

Stop laughing. This is serious.

I said, stop laughing. You're not taking this serious, Mr. Phillips.

Oh no? Well, you're wrong—this is very serious. What you did was a crime, and I want to see that justice is dealt to you swiftly and severely. And I expect to hold you here indefinitely or at least until the police arrive, which should be any minute now.

Yes, I called the police.

No, they didn't laugh at me too.

I have to say of all the people in our neighborhood, you have been by far the most unfriendly neighbor. Since the day we moved in, you've had it out for me. And I don't know what I could have done to—

That is not true—I did not shimmy up your drainpipe and poop in your gutter.

No, I didn't—and no, I don't know who did it, but it certainly wasn't me. I'm five foot five and 160 pounds. I can barely do one pull-up for the presidential fitness test. The gym teacher just shakes her head at me. She thinks I don't know what she's thinking. But I know. It's not my fault that my mom made me French bread pizzas for breakfast. I've been a victim my whole childhood, Mr. Phillips, and you're just another one of them determined to victimize me.

Don't you dare move, Tom. Sorry . . . don't you dare move, Mr. Phillips. Just what drives a man to throw a child's bike into the trees like that? I haven't thrown your car into the tree.

Damn right . . . *darn* right, I've thought about it. But I
haven't because A) I'm not strong enough, B) I failed my
driving test, and C) I'm an upstanding citizen of the United
States of America. There is something called the code of
decency, Mr. Phillips. I doubt you've heard of it. My mother
complains about it all the time, so I know it's a big problem.
Doesn't surprise me you don't follow it . . . I just mean that
what you did wasn't decent. You know that bike isn't just to
get me from point A to point B, right? It's to help me lose
weight. You are now responsible for me being fat—are you
okay with that responsibility? Huh?

It was not blocking your car. Lie after lie. I will not take this
libel from you. Or slander, whatever. Get out of my mind,
Mr. Phillips—you're manipulating me. You're manipulating
a defenseless fat child, violating my basic rights as a human
being, and breaking the law by vandalizing my property.

Does it matter if I *just* learned about citizen's arrest in class?
What does that have to do with anything? You're the
monster. Don't wave me off. I don't care if you're late to
work—you'll have to run me over before I let you past.

No, don't you dare start up the engine. Help! Help! I'm
being assaulted. If you don't stop, Mr. Phillips, I'm going
poop in your drainpipe again . . .

[*Beat.*]

Crap.

Stepson Returns

Gina Nicewonger

TILT, 11 to 13

TILT is a middle-school student on a mission to visit his former stepmom, Debbie. When Debbie was his stepmom, TILT did not make life easy for her. Her serious attitude conflicted with TILT's main goal in life, which was to have fun. He wanted to eat junk food, skip doing his homework, and, above all, swim in a pool that had a water slide. At the time, he didn't think Debbie could ever compare with his mom, but in the past six months, he has come to realize that he misses her and that she may have had something valuable to offer after all. TILT is standing outside of Debbie's house and has just rung her doorbell.

TILT   Oh good! This is your house. It's so great to see you, Debbie. I'm sorry if it's weird for me to stop by. I know you and my dad aren't married anymore, so you shouldn't have to put up with me. I saw your forwarding address in my dad's phone and I wanted to tell you that I miss you, Debbie.

I know. I can't believe I'm saying that, either! And I'm not going to ask for money or anything. I just wanted to say hey. It wasn't so bad having someone make me do my homework and yell at me for eating too many Cheetos. Truth is, I'm back on the Cheetos. It's just hard when you're not around.

And, I know you said the divorce didn't have anything to do with me, but I also didn't make things easy. I did ruin your cappuccino machine trying to make hot chocolate. I had to! You barely ever used it!

[*Calming himself.*]

The point is, I was wrong. And, it wasn't fair when I compared you to my mom. We all know she's not perfect either, and you were a pretty good mom. God, I bet you're so happy to be rid of me. I mean, look at this place. It's great. Is that a pool there in the back?

No, I did not come over to use your pool, Debbie. I didn't even know you had a pool. The fact that I'm wearing swim trunks is a coincidence.

And, accusing me of using you for your pool sounds like something you would do. Oh my god. You just get me so steamed up, Debbie. You're making this so hard. It doesn't have to be that way!

[*Taking a breath.*]

Let's just let this all go and do something fun.

Yeah, like swim in your pool! What would be so bad about me swimming in your pool? You have this perfectly good pool and no one is swimming in it, Debbie. I mean god, you always have the best stuff and you never use any of it!

Sorry. We've been here before, haven't we? All right Debbie, I'll leave you alone. But I know you miss me, too. I know because you rented the one house in this whole neighborhood with a water slide. Every time you don't use it, I bet you think of me. I'll hold that here forever, Debbie.

[*Signaling to his heart.*]

I'll hold that here forever.

Confession

Alessandra Rizzotti

JOE, 16 to 18

JOE sits in an interrogation room at the police station. He is washed-up and angry at an early age.

JOE I met Jeff playing football in the parking lot of the Cosabella Royale Apartments in Tucson, Arizona, after I got emancipated. My mom was like super drunk all the time, so I had to get out. He was a free spirit, like me. Totally not willing to be parented anymore. We moved in together shortly after because I was kinda new to the area and didn't really have any friends. I was trying to get away from the chaos of the fucking high school that made me suicidal. So anyway, we move right next to a German shepherd named Shiba Rula Guantanamo Bay and Fred—I don't know his last name—but he was a professional bowler who later became a computer programmer. He was cool. He got us beer from the liquor store because we didn't have our fake IDs yet. . . . Wait—you won't arrest Fred, right? I don't have a fake ID anymore, I swear.

Anyways, Jeff said he couldn't pay rent that third month, so I made him move out. It was okay, though, and we stayed friends despite the weirdness because he found a place across the street where this old lady lived. It was this adobe house that he called the "spook house" because he was sure her dead husband haunted the place, rolling around in his wheelchair backwards. He even did impersonations of it at parties because it was so funny. Imagine him spooking. Jeff moved in with this girl named Carol, and I swear, something about her seemed fishy. He'll tell you he should have married her. But man, it was hard to ever see him because of her. She was needy. But needy in the possessive, manipulative, you-can't-have-friends way. She was like, older than us, you know? Like almost date rapey. I don't even really know the age of Jeff, though, so who knows, maybe he just said he was young like me so I'd let him move in?

I had this meteorologist move into Jeff's old room. His brother would come over and they'd drink frozen strawberry daiquiris like some gay dudes. But you know, the meteorologist got married and had a baby who had water in the brain, so that went to shit. I mean, everything was just going to shit. I fell in love with a lady who reminded me of my mom—she was named Ramona and I cheated on her with someone my own age—I swear it wasn't my fault. I mean it was, but Ramona and I had agreed to be more free-spirited and stuff, so I thought it was okay. The love is still strong and it hurts.

Anyways, you don't want to hear this stuff. I don't really know what to say to you, because to hear Jeff is now a murderer is kinda mind-blowing. Something in me says he didn't do it. You know, he was about to go to the air force he said. Totally out of character. But he did things that surprised me. Like, he was fluent in German. He wasn't a Nazi, though. We used to have parties in Tucson and play Motown all night long. We'd have tons of girls over.

He's innocent. He has to be. He was more of a brother to me than my actual brother. That says something. I value who he is. I don't think anyone else would say differently. I mean, he just took care of a friend's dad and helped our old neighbor's business by manning the register when the guy had a heart attack. I mean, he's always there. Shit . . . do you think he feeds off of old people? He acts all nice to get close and then he murders them? Shit . . . I never realized that. There is a part of me that knows this guy is a mystery. He's friendly, but always distant in a way. Goddamn me. I trust everyone. By accident. Sometimes. God knows Ramona can't trust me, but I trust her—and I trust everyone she knows. By default. To a fault. Fuck. I'm so dumb!

You think he did it, don't you? He's a real suspect, isn't he? I should have never given him my bike rack. That blood will never come off, will it?

D&D Dating

Carla Cackowski

OWEN, 15

A 15-year-old boy is on a first date.

OWEN   So, yeah, this is the basement. And, uh, here's the couch. You can take a seat. Here. By me. I mean, only if you want.

[*They sit.*]

Yeah, the movie was funny. Thanks for paying for your own ticket. My mom gave me enough money to buy your ticket, too, but thanks for being cool about it so I could buy popcorn and soda instead.

Oh sure. I would totally take you out again. Yeah. Sitting next to each other and watching a movie and not having to really talk, that wasn't so bad. I just mean, there wasn't too much pressure. It was easy, is all. You're very easy. Not like that! You know what I mean.

So, I bet you're wondering why I brought you down to my basement . . .

[*He moves closer to her.*]

Here's the thing, Grace. I really like you a lot. And I want to do something with you that I've never done with a girl before. Grace, how do you feel about . . . [*He leans in.*] playing Dungeons and Dragons with me?

[*Super suave.*]

My buddies and I, see, we don't ask just anyone into our inner circle. But you're special, Grace. You're very special. From the moment you cornered me after biology and said, "Are you going to take me out on a date, or what?" I knew that you were exactly the type of aggressive, take-no-prisoners, badass pixie that we've been searching for to join us on our journey.

You don't want to be a pixie? . . . How about an elf? A gnome? Fairy? Too girly? I know! What about a monk?! Wait, Grace, please. Just listen.

[*Leans in again.*]

I really need you . . . to help us take down the Beast Shaman. His supernatural powers are kicking our asses. If you were a pixie, you would have spell resistance, the capability to create dancing lights, make ghost sounds, protect yourself with invisibility. Grace. If you joined us as a pixie, you would be polymorphic!

[*Follows after her.*]

I really don't understand what about this situation isn't appealing to you?

[*His friends enter.*]

Oh, hey guys! Grace, this is Lord Cruamors, Adele the Rogue, Hortifice the Drover, and Montepuss the Barbarian. You guys, perfect timing! I was just explaining to Grace how we've never played D&D with a girl before and we're real excited to have her here so we can get the feminine perspective on battling the Beast Shaman, not to mention our impending battle with the Hybrid Elite Warrior in Goblin Valley.

Grace, please don't leave! You can't! I promised everyone you'd play. Grace. Please. Sure, my friends are here now, but we, you and I . . . well, we're on a date.

You'll stay? She'll stay, you guys! [*They cheer.*] Don't wanna be a pixie? No problem! Take a look at the handbook and pick something else. [*To friends.*] I know, right? Told you guys she was awesome. [*To Grace.*] So, what'd you decide? A swashbuckler. You really want to be a swashbuckler? Grace, this is serious stuff. Swashbucklers are daring adventurers who combine courage, skill, resourcefulness, chivalry, and a distinctive sense of honor and justice. You up for that? [*Smiles at her response.*] This is the best date I've ever been on. I mean, sure, it's the first date I've ever been on, but . . . It. Is. Awesome. It means a lot to me that you stayed.

Don't call me that. Aidan isn't here right now. You can call me Ogrete the Dauntless.

You'll Shoot Your Eye Out (and I'll Laugh)

Andy Goldenberg

BOBBY FRIEDMAN, 16

BOBBY FRIEDMAN, a 16-year-old kid, has just watched his younger brother open up the birthday gift—a toy rifle—that BOBBY has given him. This has all happened in front of BOBBY's parents.

BOBBY FRIEDMAN   No, you're right, Mom. It's an unsuitable present . . . for any child. The Magic Bang Bang Ping Pong Lucky Lou Sawed-Off Shotgun should probably not be played with by anyone under the age of eighteen. I mean, look at it. It has a firing mechanism that contains a gas that's ignited by a spark every time you pull the trigger. That is just asking for trouble. Plus, it clearly states that this product is unsuitable for kids. Right there, on the box, huge letters. But as a teenager, let me just say that no matter WHAT my little brother asked for, trouble would find him. The whole GOAL of being an adolescent boy is to fuck up as much shit—MESS up as much STUFF—as possible and see what you can and can't get away with. Can I hit my brother in the face and not get punished? Can I jump to the ground from my bedroom window and not break my neck? Can I touch Monica McDonald's boobs and not get killed? You have your answers, but I'm a curious cat and I need to figure things out for myself. It only stands to reason, then, that Mikey over here CAN and WILL make ANY present unsuitable. Give him a teddy bear, and he'll whip it around like it was a battle-axe. Give him a jump rope, and he'll use it as a lasso or choke someone with it. Give him underwear . . . [*He shudders.*] . . . and you better believe he'll wear it on the outside of his clothing just to embarrass you. He's a boy. It's what we do. We like danger and we're attracted to getting in trouble. The key, then, is to give him NOTHING. Now hear me out. You take back all of your gifts—save you some money and some heartache down the line—and I will take back mine . . . or keep it . . . whatever. [*To Mikey.*] Oh, you poor baby with your first world problems. [*Back to parents.*] Let him cry about how he never gets anything. How nobody ever listens to him because he's the youngest. How I get so many presents on MY birthday because I have more friends and I'm cooler and my voice doesn't sound like a girl. Let him cry. Because you both gave him the greatest gift of all . . . LIFE! Right? Wasn't such a walk in the park for YOU, was it? And I know how Mom can be when she's NOT pregnant. Listen . . . Mikey can be an ungrateful little snot. I know this. I had to share a bedroom with the disgusting little troll until just a few years ago. [*To Mikey.*] They gave you the ability to walk and talk and look halfway like a normal human being and you're going to be upset because you don't get some stupid action figure that's bendable and poseable? Kids today, right? They're so unappreciative.

Sheena Isn't a Punk Rocker

Meg Swertlow

JACKSON, late teens

JACKSON is in his late teens, is super hip (like really, really hip), and is really into "being hip" (like really, really into it).

JACKSON   I'm sorry, but if your band isn't influenced by the Ramones, then your band is bullshit. My band Sheena Is: A Sellout was obviously influenced by the Ramones, which means it's definitely not bullshit.

Cool name for a band, right? Yeah named them myself. I just thought, "Well, Sheena may have been a punk rocker, but if she were alive today, she'd totally be a sellout." I mean sometimes I think it's probably a good thing Kurt Cobain killed himself when he did. If he were alive today to see what kind of shit music was being produced, he'd probably kill himself.

People always ask me, "What Ramone are you most like, Jackson?" I always thought of myself as a DeeDee Ramone type—you know, behind the scenes, making stuff happen. But who am I kidding? I really need to come into my own power and take ownership of who I am. I'm the Joey of the group, the leader, the one in charge, the tallest. I am like Joey, with way better teeth and not dead.

See this tattoo on my right forearm? [*Points to forearm.*] . . . That's Joey Ramone, riding on the back of a stallion. And see this tattoo? [*Points to the left forearm.*] . . . That's a stallion riding on the back of Joey Ramone. I'm sure you already know this—but the stallion is the symbol for Sire Records, the Ramones' record label/captors for fifteen years. The whole thing is a metaphor for the tyranny of the record industry.

Fine! Don't believe me, what do I know?! I'm just the most important man in the music! I'm kidding. Actually I am not—my dad always said "project for the life you want to have"—he should know . . . he's assistant to the booking agent at the Staples Center.

What I'm trying to say is—maybe today I am not "the most important man in music"—but I will be. Once Sheena Is: A Sellout puts out an EP, and after I'm done with this unpaid internship at Sire Records that my dad said he's gonna get for me. I think once that stuff happens—it's my time.

Anyway—so yeah, to answer your question: The Ramones are my favorite band.

Oh, you didn't ask me that? Ooooh, what am I getting for dinner? The steak tacos.

I'm really glad we went on this date, you seem chill . . . what was your name?

Plastic Revolution

Mark Alderson

ROGER, 13

ROGER, *a young but clear-faced teenager, is addressing his peers and standing on the bench inside a local ice-cream parlor.*

ROGER Okay guys, thanks for seeing me here. I know the Frosty Freeze isn't the best place to meet, but my mom is doing holiday shopping next door and she's my ride.

I know what you're all thinking. We don't need to do this. Well, we do. We are thirteen years old and the time has come for us to become men.

No more playing with action figures. Yes, I know it will be tough, but the rewards will be *awesome*. I mean, who wouldn't want to trade their super-chopping action hero for a driver's license? Or pass on our Warrior Quest cards to our younger siblings for a date with Chelsea Quinn from homeroom! It's time to start acting our age, friends.

Let me tell you the good news, though! This is only temporary. We can collect our action figures and hero cards when we hit our midlife crisis. Men all over the world are doing it! Just the other day I saw a vintage Pocket Monster card on Ebidz.com, so I know that we are not alone. YOU are not alone. Because any time we feel the urge to buy the latest Spaceborg Power Blaster, just know how much cooler it will be to kiss Chelsea Quinn. By the way, I am only using her as an example for this scenario. We all know that she let me borrow a pencil last week, so we are basically on the fast track to love.

So boys . . . ahem . . . MEN! Let's drop our plastic toys and pick up our newfound freedom. Who's with me!

[*The crowd cheers.*]

Now, who can give me a ride home? My mom just texted me and said she's going to be running late and I don't want to walk home alone—it's scary.

What Are You Packing?

Kathy S Yamamoto

PETER, 16

PETER is a teenager who has a little too much swagger. He's the kind of guy who would rather pretend he knows what everyone else is talking about instead of asking for an explanation.

PETER   Hey bros! Sorry I'm late—my mom would not stop talking to our neighbor. I was like, "C'mon, Mom! I'm gonna be late for practice!" [*Calls off to stands.*] Moms, am I right?

Anyway, you guys ready to play some ball? Randall, you gotta step up your game, bro, if we're gonna beat Chester High. Your jump shot is all over the place, bro! Why you guys laughing?

Did you just say you're packing eight inches? Are you trying to brag? Dude, that is tiny, you should get that checked out—I don't think that's normal. Eight inches is not big, dude. Eight inches is nothing, I have twelve inches on me!

Brandon, don't look so surprised. Twelve inches is actually super normal. What isn't normal is all the crumbs you get from it. I feel like there's crumbs everywhere, dog! In my lap, on the floor. There's a little trail of crumbs falling from my pants wherever I go. I'm like Hansel and Gretel, but you know, with much more swag. Yeah, ever since it got dry outside, I feel like there's more crumbs and I'm all, get outta here crumbs. Crumbs, am I right?

Why do you guys look so surprised? What size is yours? Mmm . . . now you're all quiet, huh? Man, maybe twelve inches is only normal in my family. We're all big eaters, you know what I'm saying?

Even my sister is packing twelve inches these days. Yeah, that's kind of weird, I gotta admit, but you know, I respect her choices. She's almost twelve now, and I feel like she can do what she wants, you know? She's not a baby anymore.

[*Jordan looks at* PETER *in shock.*]

Jordan. Close your mouth, you look like an idiot. If you don't close your mouth, I'm gonna stuff my twelve inches in it! Ha-ha! You'd be a lucky dude, but don't worry, I won't. It's all mine.

[*Frankie says something.*]

Of course I'm going to eat it myself, don't be an idiot, Frankie! Who else is going to do it? Tracy? Please, that chick does not deserve one inch, not to mention my twelve inches! She'd be lucky to have that.

Although, can we have real talk for a minute. Like, I am happy with the twelve inches I'm packing, but like, do you think it's weird if it has a meaty smell? I mean, I'm used to a weird smell, but this meaty smell is new . . . like it almost smells salty. I mean, I haven't put meat in anything for years, so you know it makes me think that something is not clean down there. Yeah, maybe I should just get it checked out.

[*Luke says something.*]

What do you mean, prove it? You think I'm lying Luke? You think I'd make up the twelve inches in my sack? How could you say I'm a liar—we've been friends since Ms. Kimbrel's life science class in the fourth grade. You're going to throw that away because you think I'm lying? When have I ever lied to you in my life?

Fine, I'll prove it. Here, take a look.

[*He pulls out a twelve-inch sandwich from his pants.*]

See? Check it! Twelve whole inches. I even measured it when I was at Subway. There were all those reports on how Subway was cheating everyone, giving them ten inches instead of twelve inches, and I was like, that ain't cool. So now I always check to make sure that they give me twelve inches of bread.

Why y'all laughing? What were you guys talking about? Oh, your penises? Oh, then yeah, my penis is twelve inches long.

A Formal Presentation

JP Karliak

COREY, 15 to 18

COREY *and his best friend, Brendan, are playing video games in* COREY'*s basement. Brendan casually brings up the topic of the winter formal, but to* COREY, *there is nothing casual about a formal.*

COREY   No, Brendan, I don't know who I'm taking yet.

Buddy, I'm well aware the dance is a week away, but there are multiple factors to consider. Not just any girl or guy will do. Yes, I'm considering both genders equally—it diversifies my options.

Like? Brendan, it doesn't matter who I like. I'm not physically attracted to a single person in our class. Not one. And the reason is very simple: we grew up together. These are the same people from kindergarten who explosively crapped themselves during recess. Rubbed ranch dressing on their faces. Ate nickels. And that's mostly the girls. Sure, they've developed curves since then, but I can't remove the image of them as barely more than toddlers leaking profusely from the eyes and nose—it's burned into my brain. And the guys . . . well, you know, male puberty and locker-room behavior is just a horror movie. Like online ones from Russia. It's sick.

Of course I'm still going! Yeah, it'll be a night without romance, but there are other benefits to attending the winter formal. Picture our classmates ten or twenty years from now, pulling out the old yearbook, flipping through, feeling nostalgic. They'll get to the picture of me and my date, and they'll think very specific thoughts. Was my date good-looking, did I "level up," does it make them a little jealous? Or maybe I went with somebody considerably less attractive, and then they remember I was a decent guy for "taking one for the team." And let's also consider not just what my date is like now but also who they'll likely become. If in ten years, they're a serial killer or a presidential candidate, those will produce very different reactions to our portrait. Well, at least slightly different. Without any romantic entanglements, I think it'd be imprudent not to consider all variables.

Okay, let's start with the girl shortlist: Hannah Prendergast. Pretty, we've been friends since second grade and we get along well, so I'll look like I'm having fun, which is key to good pictures. But she has very few aspirations beyond staying local and having babies, so in the long run, I dunno if that'd make people think I was remarkable for taking her. Grace is gorgeous, but will make every photo about herself and probably won't stick around long enough to get one with me in it. Olivia starts out pretty but dances too hard and becomes a sweaty mess. Sam is top of the class and is probably going to be something awesome in politics, but she makes a weird duck-lips selfie face in every single picture.

The guy list is shorter, 'cause you have to find one that actually wouldn't mind going with another guy. There's Carter, who definitely would, but he's so huggy that everybody would assume we've been secretly a couple for years and would look at a picture thinking, "Aw, they were so cute, too bad they didn't stay together." I don't even know his last name. There's also Eric, who's very smart, but he'd dictate every detail of the night. I hate people that overplan. Plus his eyebrows are too nice.

Ugh, it's so hard, though! Ya know what'd make it stupidly easy? If you and I just went together. I mean, think about it: we've been best friends since daycare, so we wouldn't have to explain anything—they'd just think we were buddies having a good time. Which we would be! We could even get a stupid prom pic together, and years from now, when I'm getting my award from *Forbes* or you're getting yours from . . . I dunno, *Field & Stream* . . . they'll show that great picture of us and reference how we both went on to great things! Great successful friends! They could even use that one of us from Grace's pool party last year, where we kissed during Truth or Dare. I mean, it's just such a random funny picture of two guys who love each other. As friends. Great friends. Or more than friends. Like brothers!

Of course I'm serious! Why, do *you* have a date already?

Hannah. I see. Well, Brendan, to be honest, I think you lack vision.

Therapy Breakup

Gina Nicewonger

GRANT, 16 to 18

GRANT *wears his heart on his sleeve and thinks every girl is "the one." However, he's never had a real relationship for longer than a year. He's broken it off with many girls.* GRANT *thought therapy might help in his search for love, so he started seeing Dr. Jill Mitchell over a year ago. He thinks his therapist is good at her job, but like all his romantic relationships, he believes he and the therapist are missing the "magic" needed to be effective.* GRANT *wants to follow Dr. Mitchell's advice of "trying something different" and has come to her office to tell her in the only way he knows how he won't be returning to therapy.*

GRANT   Listen, we need to talk. I know we always talk, but we need to really talk. Don't you hate those words? They're almost as bad as, "It's not you. It's me." But in this case, it's not you. It's totally me.

[*She speaks.*]

I guess I can't hide anything from you. I'm awfully sorry, but yeah, I'm breaking it off with you.

[*Moved.*] This is what makes it so hard. You know me so well. And you get me.

[*She speaks.*]

I know I didn't have to come down here to tell you that we can't be together anymore. I know. But come on. We've been seeing each other for four years. I'm a better guy than that.

[*She speaks.*]

[*Smiling.*] No, no, no. I DO understand that you're my therapist and that our relationship is "strictly professional." But, Dr. Mitchell, I don't know if you understand how much you've helped me get through some really tough times.

[*Laughs.*] God. We've had some good times, haven't we?

[*She speaks.*]

Jill, I've got to stop you right there. Is it okay if I call you Jill?

[*She speaks.*]

Stick with Dr. Mitchell? Fine. Dr. Mitchell, do you know I've been seeing you longer than I've seen any other woman? You're so encouraging, but at the same time you see through all of my bullshit. And the best part: you always laugh at my jokes. God, I'm going to miss your laugh.

[*She speaks.*]

I'm sorry. I must be coming off as a crazy person. And, I'm trying to tell you that you're so good at your job. I'd hate for you to think I'm just now becoming crazy!

[*She laughs.*]

There's that laugh. You're an amazing person. But, sometimes you just got a branch out and try something different. Someone very wise once told me that.

[*Getting emotional.*] God Brian, don't get choked up now. Change is hard. I think I told you that one. But hey, we're both going to be okay.

[*She speaks.*]

Oh, you better. I'm going to treasure the invoice for this session for a long, long time. Please. Think of me fondly.

Craven Saint Todd

Brandon Econ

CRAVEN SAINT TODD, 14 to 18

CRAVEN SAINT TODD *would prefer not to discuss the period in time prior to his being sired and taken into to the cult of Nosferatu. His entrance into this world was fraught with much darkness and light—mostly light and light burns (get it away, get it away, hiss, hiss!). And please do not bring up his two older brothers, Van Saint Todd and Helsing Saint Todd; they always tease him and steal his black eye shadow (which* CRAVEN *steals from ULTA, but still . . .).* CRAVEN *loves anything by Anne Rice and enjoys eating Nutter Butters while hanging upside down from the rafters, which he can only do for so long before the blood of his victims (maybe?) rushes to his head. Here,* CRAVEN *is talking to his new neighbors, Chris and Susan Brown, on their doorstep.*

CRAVEN SAINT TODD   I hope I'm not interrupting. I saw you unloading boxes, so I figured I'd stop by.

Hi, nice to meet you. I'm Craven Saint Todd. I'm a vampire. Well not really, but, you never know. Oh wow, Chris and

Susan Brown. What a great name for both of you. Wow, yeah. Lemme give you the rundown. Well, so this IS a really family-oriented community, it's pretty quiet around here normally. It's really great you know. But sometimes me and my brood have these monthly gatherings. I wanted to make sure that you knew that. I don't want to get started on the wrong foot. You know. The person that lived here before, total ass. I mean, he would call the police on us every time we would have our simulated slayings. It got really bad morale-wise. We would plan things months in advance, you know. Find an actor on LA Casting and everything. So I just wanted to let you know that we do that sometimes.

Oh, yeah, it's this thing we do. Well, we just run through the neighborhood and chase down an actor, corner her, and then drain her life force. I mean not really, but, usually.

I just had a thought. You and Susan should totally come over for dinner one night. Well, yeah, when you get settled in. I love to entertain new guests. I make some of the best Mexican food. You would think I was a real Mexican instead of a vampire. I mean, yeah. You two could stick around and I could introduce you to my cohorts. Usually every first Tuesday of the month we have a traditional Mexican dinner and masquerade ball in my backyard. We all dance and drink and listen to Gregorian chants. You know, just relax and share in the joys of being a member of the living dead. I mean not really, but, well? So that would be fun. You would be surprised how . . .

Oh, you have a cat—put it away! Put it away! I'm just joking, you know. Well you have to lighten up a little, Chris. Me and my coven do that sort of thing all the time. Some of us get really into it. I remember last week. Alana brought over real human blood. Well it was Pinot Noir, but you know what I mean. We were passing it around like in a real blood-rite and some of us just, you know, went on a rampage in the community and were jumping on cars and chasing children and I found a rock and I threw it. It got really crazy. When I woke up the next morning, I had wine stains all over my jabot. You have no idea how difficult it is to get that out. We just really let loose. But we have a lot of fun, really. Really!

Well, I've talked your ear off nonstop. I better let you get back to unpacking. It was nice talking to you, and think about my offer. We'll probably see each other again. Like in the middle of the night when I'm standing over your bed ready to suck you dry. I'm only kidding, but, well, maybe. Bye.

The "Teaching" Breakup

Brendan McCay

DUSTIN, 16 to 19

DUSTIN *is a male teen who is frustrated, patronizing, and overly confident. Here, he attempts to "win" a breakup and save some face by "helping" his soon-to-be ex-girlfriend by giving unsolicited advice. Instead, however, he digs himself into a hole of self-righteousness.*

DUSTIN   Look, you are honestly the sweetest girl I've met in a long time. I love hanging out with you—I just don't think the relationship part is going so well . . .

You tried to make out with me during *Finding Nemo!* There were kids in the audience cheering on Nemo to find his dad while you were trying to see what you could do to my little Nemo! That is a really hard place to put me in! No pun intended. GOSH. Do you see what you do to me? I just need you to understand that I can't continue seeing you romantically. And since I am being completely honest here . . . I hate your lip gloss. HATE IT. Why would you choose "Cake Batter" flavored lip gloss? Every time we make out I am vividly brought back to my fifth birthday party, when my mom dropped the cake on my unwrapped presents. I had to throw out TWO treasure trolls, Naomi. TWO TREASURE TROLLS.

I don't even understand why you would wear lip gloss in the first place. It's like kissing two sticky slugs, and then, when you least expect it, a third slimy slug attempts to join the party. I'm not saying you are a bad kisser, but COME ON! Ease up off of the tongue, Naom-Gnomes! I feel like you are always trying to knock my teeth out like whack-a-mole or something. Then, when you are done poking around, you do this thing where you are like licking the back of my teeth. I can't—I just can't.

Hey, don't cry! I'm not trying to be rude or anything, just trying to be honest, you know? I just feel like we are trying to shove a round peg into a square hole . . . except the peg is your tongue and the hole is my mouth . . . And it's uncomfortable. I wouldn't be telling you any of this if I didn't think it would help your future relationships. I mean, Sterling would date you in a heartbeat! If you do date Sterling, though, you will definitely need to burn the majority of your wardrobe. I don't know what his female clothing preferences are—but it can't possibly be overalls. Oh—don't look so surprised! You showed up at my parents' house last Sunday in overalls, and it looked like I picked you up from FarmersOnly.com. The only people that should be wearing overalls are plumbers from the 1980s and Old MacDonald! I don't even know where you found a pair of adult-size overalls! For as horny as you are, you would think you would know better than to show up dressed like Dennis the Menace!

Hey, wait a second, I know I've been talking a lot—it's just that I've had these things on my mind for a long time. Not that long—just for a few days since I decided I wanted to enhance slash save your future love life. I mean if you think about it—when you are dating someone, you are either going to marry that person or break up with them . . . so . . . you might as well chalk this one up as experience—right?!

I've learned a ton from dating you!

I've learned that I don't want to date someone whose best friend is their mom. I will forevermore avoid any girl who plays soccer competitively, because—y'all are crazy. And now I know I could never be with a German.

Okay. Now it can be your turn to tell me what you've learned. And don't worry, we can have one last kiss and I can give you feedback after.

Picking Up Mackinsey

Kim Mulligan

TYLER, 15 to 17

TYLER, *a nice teenage guy, is all dressed up to pick up his first date. He approaches the door, almost knocks, and then backs away.*

TYLER What am I going to say? I didn't plan this part. Her dad is probably going to answer. Come on Tyler, just play it cool.

[TYLER *takes a deep breath and does a practice run.*]

Yo, Mr. Wheeler. Oh, Swerve! Your crib is tite. I'm here for your first born. Where Mackinsey at? We gonna kill it on dat dance floor. Turn up!

[TYLER *throws up a fake gang sign and poses cool. Then shakes out.*]

What father wants that guy picking up his daughter?! Okay, I got this.

[TYLER *stands up very straight and fixes his collar looking serious. He begins speaking in a high-class affectation.*]

Good evening to you, Mr. Wheeler. I hope I have found you in good spirits and good health. I have come to accompany the young Mackinsey to the festivities this fine evening. I shall return her to you before you withdraw to your sleeping quarters.

[TYLER'*s posture falls apart.*]

What was that? Apparently, it's the eighteenth century. Hashtag, I suck at life.

[*He tries again very smoothly.*]

Hola, señor Wheeler. Yo estoy aqui accompañar Mackinsey al baile esta noche.

[TYLER *has horrified himself.*]

Derp! I am definitely not the most interesting man anywhere. This is useless.

[TYLER *lets out a deep sigh, which turns into Darth Vader breathing.*]

[*Like Darth Vader.*] Mr. Wheeler. You are Mackinsey's father. Impressive. Most impressive. Now release her.

[TYLER *reaches his hand out in front of him and tries to use "The Force" to choke an imaginary opponent. He drops it.*]

I have been trying to use The Force my whole life—why would it start working tonight. Ugh! It's like I don't even have a brain in my head sometimes.

[TYLER *gets zombified.*]

Brains! Mackinsey, brains.

[TYLER *returns to normal.*]

It's like I think of Mackinsey and I totally forget how to be a normal human.

[TYLER *gets robotic, complete with sound effects.*]

I am a normal hu-man. Hello, Mr. Wheeler, I am here to take your normal hu-man daughter, Mackinsey, to the dance tonight. We will dance like this [*Robot dancing.*], and at the conclusion of our date, if I am a lucky hu-man, we will kiss like this.

[TYLER *has his eyes closed while he robot-kisses the air. He freezes when the real door opens. Mr. Wheeler stands there.* TYLER *unrobots himself with defeated sound effects.*]

Hi Mr. Wheeler, I was just. I um, what? Yes, I like *Star Wars*, thanks for asking. Is Mackinsey home?

Baby Daddy in Prison

Alessandra Rizzotti

SEMAJ, 16 to 18

SEMAJ *sits in his prison cell after a visit from his girlfriend. He is talking to his cellmate.*

SEMAJ Man, why do women gotta be buggin'? My girl is gettin' on me for not being able to get out o' lockdown for my baby's first birthday. She's all in my lunch tryin' to figure out what I do here all day. You know we don't do nothin'. She want me to bake a cake or somethin'? Blow up balloons? I'm about to jump the couch!

[*He sighs, plopping down on the bed, staring at the ceiling.*]

Her mama sayin' we shouldn't have this baby, but I know we's able to do it. Shit, I don' never knew my dad. I'm not perfect or nothin', but I have a lot o' love to give. At least I gonna get to know this baby. I would give up my Sega Game Gear for a new baby carriage, ya know? Wheat bread instead of Cheetos, right? No more Red Bull. Just milk, right? They say you have to be healthy and shit when you gonna be raisin' babies, so I gon' have to stop hittin' up 7-Eleven for dem frozen dinners and breakfast burritos. I'll prob'ly sell my skateboard so I can get dem diapers, too.

Life's about payin' the bills, and when you don't, you go put yo'self out on the street. I ain't here because I wanted to. I was just survivin'. My brotha said I could go do a deal, and then the po-po showed in the hood right when I got there. Shiiit. I'll be out when the baby is like one and a half, though. At least it's not ten years, right?

Man, what are you in here for? Ohhhhh duuude, I forgot. You prob'ly won't see your kids ever again . . . woah . . . I didn't mean to offend you or nothin' in sayin' that, but truth's the truth.

[*He pauses and looks over his shoulder.*]

Thanks for not beatin' my ass when I said that.

When you have babies and shit, you gotta be calm and not get angry or nothin', just like you right now starin' at the ceilin' like it's some kinda blingin' Jesus on a cross. My baby mama was telling me just now how she saw a g-ma yell at her grandkid for not wearing socks and it's like, babies don't put on socks by themselves, so why are you yellin'? We would never yell at our baby. No way. We is goin' to talk like she is loved. We's gonna tell her she is a princess and that she gonna grow up to be a hair stylist, or whatevah. I don't know math or nothin', but I would git her in school so she could learn it. My uncle and me, we deal with numbers in our business, but I wouldn't want the baby mixed in that. D.A.R.E. to keep babies off the streets, ya know? Ha-ha.

I should learn from my mistakes, but I don't know how else to make money at this point. What do you do after you get out of here? Oh wait, you prob'ly don't care.

My baby mama is trying to get her GRE. She's smarter than me. Well, obviously. She ain't here. Ha. Oh lord, please help me get out of here so I can start ovah. It's harder to be a person than to create one, ya know what I mean?

Hey—you listenin'?

[*He turns back to his cellmate.*]

Yo, you always be dissin' me, fallin' asleep when I'm talkin'. You wack.

Anyway

Jeff Bogle

CHAD O'BRIEN, 17

The scene begins midday, just outside a trendy alt-culture/ punk-clothing store in the local suburban mall, and continues as CHAD and his 16-year-old friend are walking around the corner to the food court. By the end of the scene, the two are seated, munching on their fast-food lunches.

CHAD   It's so rad to have my own wheels. My girlfriend lives about twenty minutes away from my parent's house and I spend tons of time there. Also, Burger King. Man, those Chicken Cordon Blue Sandwiches are ridiculous!

Anyway, I hear you are going to be taking your driver's license exam soon. That's awesome. Remember to come to a complete stop at those Stop signs, dude. I was nearly flunked by the fascist old bag who did my test. Thankfully my dad does her taxes and he got her a huge tax return or something last year so she passed me. Phew. Oh, man, there's something else you gotta know about driving: wear shoes.

No, I'm serious. Quit laughing. They can be whatever—flip-flops, Air Jordans, Chuck Taylors, I don't care—but, dude, you've gotta have 'em on your downstairs digits, like, always.

Once, last year, I got pulled over by some bored cop near that elementary school. Yeah, the one behind where the movie theater used to be. You remember seeing *Clerks* there? Aw snap, that movie was so rad. "You snowballed him!" Anyway, I got nabbed going, like, 27 or something in a school zone. Oh, school zones are 15 miles per hour when the kids are either going or coming and the lights are blinking. But dude, it was like barely the school year, the first week of September or something. I was still on summer time, you know? Cops should give you, like, a two-week buffer or something. Had no idea those poor fools were back in prison for another nine months.

Anyway, so the cop nails me right after I'd been through the Micky D's drive-thru. I know, right! I'm munching on my McMuffin and hash brown, taking turns—McMuffin, hash brown, McMuffin, hash brown, you know, trying to make 'em come out even in the end—when the siren and lights start. Shit. I had no shoes on. What? Dude, it was like eight in the morning. I was so damn tired and hungry and just ran out real quick to get some breakfast.

Anyway, the copper wants my insurance and registration— they always ask for that stuff—and, well, did I tell you about the cool shit my girl and I did that summer? The Jersey

Shore, like a dozen concerts, and going out to dinner whenever we wanted. Hey, speaking of dinner, have you tried Friendly's new patty melt? Killer!

Anyway, I spent so much cash with my girl that I didn't have enough for my car insurance. I didn't think I'd get into an accident or anything, so who cares, right? But when you don't have insurance, the state cancels your car registration. I don't even know what car registration is actually for, but the cops want you to have it. The worst part is that when you lose that, your driver's license gets suspended. That's like the holy trinity of shit right there, bro.

Anyway, what I'm saying is, make sure you wear shoes when you drive, man, because when the cop took my keys and towed my car I had to walk all the way home in bare feet.

Puppy Love

Mike McAleer

ZACHARY, 16

ZACHARY *is a socially awkward high school student. He has friends, but he prefers to spend his weekends with his adorable lab-retriever dog. They have a special bond, but now ZACHARY needs to cautiously break the news to his human-like friend that he is thinking about "seeing someone else."*

ZACHARY   Why are you pushing me away? Why are you pushing me away? You're the one who made that cute face. The one you know I can't resist. There you go again! You are so adorable and loving and caring and good. I just love you so much. I remember the first time we met, and you were so hesitant and shy at first. But then we went to get food, and that's all it took, something magical happened. Best friends. Instantly. Remember?

At night we went to the Valley Village Park and went for a long walk together. The moon was so full and big and bright. And I remember we were both so tired you crashed on my favorite leather couch with your head on my lap as I watched that rerun of *Dog the Bounty Hunter*. Such a peaceful sleeper you are.

What? Oh now you want to give me a kiss, huh?

Whoa! That breath of yours. It's like a mix between a gym class tube sock and an elevator fart. I'm sorry, but it is. Wow! I still love you, though. Now that I think of it, maybe it is partially my fault. I'm not the perfect model of dental hygiene myself. But I don't kiss you with my full tongue either. I tell you what. Today we start fresh. Together. We're going to brush after every meal. And no more late night treats. And while we're at it, let's make it a point to bathe more too. I know you don't really like baths, but you like them more than showers, so after I'm done in the shower, I will start filling the tub with not-too-hot but not-too-cold water for you. And I'll put some of that herbal liquid wash in and let it bubble up a little. That stuff smells so good, and it makes you smell so good and your hair so unbelievably soft too. Mmmm! Damn it, now all I want to do is get you in the bathtub and wash your hair, and then dry it with a towel, first, and then use the blow-dryer so it gets really soft and fluffy, and then hug you and kiss you and squeeze you. Oh! And then we can just cuddle on the leather couch and watch our favorite movie. *Beethoven's 2nd*! What do you think? I know we're supposed to be starting fresh today, but maybe a little bacon treat too?

Ha-ha, your eyes get so big whenever I say "bacon" or "treat." You don't pay attention to anything else I'm saying—but if I say that word, your eyes get so big and I have your full attention. Right? Yes, I'm right. Okay, serious question time, and then we're going for a walk. As you know, I've been spending a lot of time by myself. A lot of time. Just you and me, actually. And I've been thinking, I don't know, maybe I am ready to pursue dating again.

Maybe with Kelly again?

Hey! Come on, good boy, where are you going?

Come back here, and let's be rational about this. You want to go for a walk? You want to go for a walk, good boy? You want a treat?

She's not allergic anymore!

Talk of Corn Stalks

Hannah Gansen

CAMERON, 14

CAMERON's father is an avid gun collector and has a plethora of historic guns. CAMERON brings one to school, the Japanese Nambu semiautomatic pistol, to show to a friend. A teacher in the hallway oversees the interaction and reports it to the principal. CAMERON is suspended and must see a therapist for his "violent ways."

CAMERON   Teenagers don't really talk . . . I mean that's what my parents say. Mom says I haven't talked to her since last August when she took me to the mall to buy me new jeans. I didn't even need new jeans, anyway—they didn't have THAT many holes. She was like, "What do you think of these?" And I was like, "I don't think about jeans." And she's like, "Well, maybe you should." I mean, come on. You don't write sweet-ass riffs by sitting around thinking about jeans.

And apparently, my dad thinks writing sweet-ass riffs is the same as just sitting around. I swear, it's like he's counting the seconds until I turn sixteen so I can drive and get a job. Last summer he made me get a pollinator job. He'd drop me off on his way to work every morning at six thirty. What an awesome summer that was.

What's a pollinator? Basically, you help the corn plants inbreed, so like the corn is really good-quality corn. You put little bags on the female-ish chute part of the corn stalk, but really early in the morning, 'cause it's all dewy and wet so there's no pollen in the air yet. It really sucks though, 'cause you gotta wear a poncho but you still get super wet and slimy from the dew and cut up by the corn leaves and there's like spiders crawling around.

Afternoon is worse. It's super hot, pollen is in the air, and it sticks to you 'cause you're sweaty. It itches, you're all yellow like the Simpsons, and you have to bend the stalks over without breaking them to put big bags on the male part on top. Then, about the third week, you have to shake the big bags off the top, cover the little bags that are covering the chute, reach underneath the bigger bag, and take off the little bag. That way the plant pollinates itself. Kind of gross. I can't wait to get out of Iowa.

But yeah, I guess teenagers just don't really wanna talk. Hey, you wanna hear this new riff I'm working on?

First Comes Love

Kathy S Yamamoto

JASON, 14

JASON *is a very neurotic young man on his first date (ever) with the love of his life. He's desperate to make it work—after all, this girl could be the love of his life! So long as he doesn't ruin the date before his mom comes to pick him up.*

JASON   Kendal! I'm so excited to be on this first date with you.

[*He goes in for a hug but changes his mind last minute to shake her hand, changes his mind again a few times until he finally settles with blowing a kiss.*]

I gotta tell you, I'm super nervous. This is my first date . . . ever. To be honest, I thought there was no way that you'd agree to go out with me, so I barely had any time to prepare. But don't worry—I did do a little research. I mean, I let my mom talk about all her first dates over dinner last night, and she's been on a bunch since the divorce went through.

Dang it!!! I should not have brought up divorce on the first date, huh? Not to say that we'll get divorced, or even get married! I mean, we're only fourteen! Who knows what'll happen. But you know, if this does go well, I'd like to put it out there that I am open to marriage, especially if it's to you.

I hope that doesn't come off creepy. My mom told me of this one guy she met on FarmersOnly.com—that's an online dating site for farmers only, I guess that's pretty obvious. Anyway, as you know, my mom is not a farmer—she's a dental hygienist—but she went on FarmersOnly.com because she figured they'd all be strapping gentlemen, whatever that means. I mean, I know what that means, but it's my mom and that's gross so I'd rather pretend I don't know what that means. Anyway, she went out with this guy, Chris, who only talked about his divorce with his ex-wife who he really loved and that really put a damper on the date. And that's what I did just now, and even though I love my parents, I promise I won't talk about their divorce for the rest of the date.

Do you watch a lot of TV? I do. Right now, I really like *The Walking Dead*. Not because of the violence, but because of how suspenseful the stories are. I just want to make it clear that I am not a violent man. I know that that's something that ladies tend to be afraid of, because murder is so prevalent for you. I know this because my mom leaves Investigation Discovery on while she cooks dinner, not because I creepily look up facts about the murder of women. I'd also like to take this time to say that I am not a murderer. I mean, unless you count that time I was walking my dog, Terry, and she got hit by a car. Though that would be manslaughter at best, or actually, dogslaughter.

Oh man, I can't believe I just brought up murder AND tried to make a joke about it! I'm so sorry. This must be the worst date you've ever been on. Don't worry, my mom won't be by to pick us up for another hour, hour and a half even! We have plenty of time to turn this date around. Not to mention that all the romcoms I watched in preparation for this date have the main girl hating the guy she meets in the beginning, only to find out that he's a great guy and they usually end up getting married!

Again, open to marriage, but not expecting it from this date.

Maybe that's it. Maybe we have to start this date with you hating me, that's what'll make us work! Okay, here's something I don't think you'll like to hear: I think jumpsuits make you look fat! There, do you hate me now?

[*Kendal starts crying.*]

Oh good. You're crying. You hate me, don't you? That's the first step. Second step is marriage! We'll end up happily ever after in no time!

[*Kendal leaves.*]

Wait, where are you going? We still have more date to get to! It has to start raining, and then I'll apologize, and then you'll forgive me, and then we'll have kids.

Look, I'm sorry for saying that. I know you love jumpsuits, and honestly, no one looks good in jumpsuits. But you know what, you're the most beautiful girl in school for me—the world, even! I've had a crush on you for forever. I remember coming to kindergarten that first day and thinking, "Wow, who is that girl on the play mat with pigtails? I like her." And that's why I pulled your pigtails that day.

I'm sorry for being weird before. I guess I was just really nervous to finally go on a date with you. I've been looking forward to this for so long. Can we start over?

Great. You know, this is going really well.

Maybe we will get married after all!

Wild Horse Hijinks

Brendan McCay

TIM, 14 to 17

TIM is the leader of his group of peers. About to get kicked out of summer camp, he takes the stand to state his case on how his cabin's rambunctious hijinks are a benefit to all campers.

TIM   Let the record state that all of the allegations against Wild Horse Cabin are true. BUT let the record ALSO state that the very acts you wish to send us home for were not detrimental to our and others' camp experience but beneficial for us and the entire Sunnyvale Camp community.

Did we sneak out after messy day at three o'clock in the morning to roll around naked in the mud pit? Yes. Were our clothes subsequently misplaced and did we sprint through the field screaming "pudding on my pee-pee!?"—Yes! But was this a, and I quote, "homosexual act of corruption"? NO. I'd like to call it a "homosocial act of camaraderie" that will create long-lasting friendships and memories for all parties involved.

Did we replace Desperado Cabin's toothpaste with IcyHot? Yes. Were there bloodcurdling screams that ranged out from Desperado Cabin in a chorus of terror? Naturally. But was this an "attempt to poison fellow campers"? By NO means! I think of it as an "attempt to promote fellowship with campers"—and now Wild Horse and Desperado have a very healthy rivalry that all developing young men should have!

As for the Leslie Hill incident—did we purposefully pee in our bathing suits during seven distinct conversations with Leslie and her friends? Yes. Was the experience for her confusing and, overall, gross? Most likely. But was this a "devious attempt to urinate on young women?" Never! Think of it more like a "different approach to uniting men and women."

[*Frankly:*] Besides, Leslie Hill is kind of a snob and she deserved it.

[*Defensively:*] Wait! Wait! Before you send us back to our boring lives back home—think about how Wild Horse Cabin has entertained and enhanced all of your lives for the better here at camp.

[*Seriously:*] Pudding on my pee-pee. Thank you.

Going Viral

Mark Alderson

THOMAS WEATHERMAN, 14

THOMAS WEATHERMAN, *a teen with his braces fresh off, is speaking right into a camera and recording.*

THOMAS WEATHERMAN   Hello all. Thank you for clicking, watching, and subscribing to my channel. Look, I'm going to be honest—I don't even know why you watch my videos. *Sometimes*, I even think of the worst video idea I can write down and film it! Sure enough, the video has eleven thousand likes the next day.

All I'm asking is that you stop watching. Please. I have a contract with VideoTube for the next two years, but I need you to stop. It's taking over my life. Maybe if you all stop watching, they will let me go free. I can't take it anymore.

Do you know how much I actually get paid? Sometimes I only get paid nine cents an hour. But then I release a video of a senior citizen falling down the stairs and it's a jackpot!

The point is, I don't care about the money. I need to be free. VideoTube is monitoring my family. Yes, I forgot to read the small print on a contract I signed and now me and my entire family is the cast of a new VideoTube reality show and is being monitored 24-7. They even got my great grandpa involved by installing a camera at his solitaire tournaments.

They will stop at nothing and I'm scared. So please, fellow subscribers and viewers. Stop watching. My safety depends on it.

Thanks! Don't forget to comment!

Hey Miss

Alessandra Rizzotti

PABLO, 13

PABLO *sits on some steps with a group of his friends, at night, watching his neighbors walk their dogs. He's the bold one of the group, not shy about talking to anyone. He clearly needs attention.*

PABLO   Hey miss, you got nice legs. Hey miss, you sexy. You should come over for a playdate. Your dog and my dog. Hey miss, are you listening?

I don't mean no disrespect. I was just admiring your beauty. I would like to take you out for a date when I'm eighteen. That will be in three years, but I figure I should let you know now since I don't want you to have any boyfriends or nothin'.

No? You don't want a date? Why not? I'm a good boy. I like giving roses to ladies. I also think my dad is going to give me his car when I can drive so that I can take you out for tacos or something.

[*Beat.*]

Miss, don't tell me how to talk to you. I am respectful. My daddy has four girlfriends, and I am JUST looking at you, so I KNOW how to treat a lady.

Miss, don't walk away. Come on. Do you know science? I need help with my chemistry homework. It's about physical and chemical properties or something and I don't know what that even means. I'm also learning sex ed and stuff. Do you know about that?

Miss, come back! My mom and dad are screaming right now and I don't want to go back inside the house. Can you talk with me?

[*Beat.*]

Yes, I'll promise to speak nicely to you. I thought I was doing that . . . okay. What is your name? How are you?

My name is Clarence. I go to school across the street. I'm fifteen. My boys live across the street. They're sixteen and twenty-one and we just like to hang out and shoot the shit and skateboard. Sorry I spoke to you earlier like that. I don't have good role models or nothing. But seriously, can you call me next year when I'm eighteen? You're so pretty . . .

Hey hey . . . sorry! I'm serious, though. Okay okay. I'll find someone my own age. They're just so boring, you know? You seem intelligent and stuff. I have things I need to learn.

I want you to teach me. Okay okay. I'll stop. See you
tomorrow, miss. I like your dog. My dog likes your dog.
They could be boyfriend and girlfriend if we can't, right?

Kick Ass, Ass-Kicker

Andy Goldenberg

STEWART, 13 to 15

STEWART, *a teenager, confronts his bully. The scene takes place in front of the bully's locker at school.*

STEWART   [*Cautiously.*] Hey Spencer.

[*Strongly flinches, as if he's about to be hit. He's not.*]

I was wondering if you were going to kick the shit out of me today. It's Friday and it's almost one forty-five, and I just need to know if you're still on schedule. It's totally fine if you want to. I understand that you have a lot of aggression and frustration that you want to take out on me. I take full responsibility for bumping into you yesterday afternoon and I have already made sure that I will never walk the same path through the building to go home. That's your path. This is your school. I respect your authority.

[*Strongly flinches again.*]

I deserve to be disciplined. I was in the wrong place at the wrong time. I also know that I am in absolutely NO position to negotiate or ask for leniency, but I feel that, as I am about to be severely handicapped from today's festivities, there could be no more harm in at least trying. Which is why I have come to your locker. And now get on my knees.

[*Takes a deep breath, ready to make his case, dropping to his knees, praying.*]

Spencer, I would appreciate it if you didn't punch my face. Not today. My parents have a very important social function tomorrow morning that I have tried several times to avoid, but they have insisted that I go. It's my birthday party, and as much as I'd love to feign illness or cancel it altogether, they've spent a lot of money securing the roller-skating rink and it's less than forty-eight hours' notice so they can't get their deposit back. And if you hit me in the face, I'll surely die. I'm slightly anemic and I bleed very easily as it is.

[*Lifts up his arm, rolls up his sleeve.*]

You see this? Someone patted me on the shoulder. Black and blue. I've had it for a week.

[*Rolls the sleeve down.*]

I shudder to think what would happen if you actually struck my face. You're the biggest kid in our grade and the only one with a full beard. Your dad owns a gym and your mom is the tallest woman I've ever met. You have to take pity on me, Spencer. I'll do your homework for you. I'll cook you lunch every day for a week. I'm already paying you the required dollar protection fee that everyone else in the class is forking over, but I can raise it since obviously my security plan doesn't cover accidental collision insurance.

[*He gets nothing from Spencer.*]

Obviously I know you're a busy man and that you have several people who need to be destroyed on a daily basis. I'm sure I'm not the only kid on your program who has come to you today looking for a break. Hell, I know Ari Alexander didn't move away. He dropped out of school and moved into some kind of middle-school witness protection program. I only ask that you take my case into consideration and grant me the one wish on my birthday cake that you have the power to control. Also, I wear glasses.

[*He feels like he's made his case as best as he can.*]

If I don't see you at three, have a great weekend and thank you for your time. Your majesty.

[*He bows humbly and leaves.*]

My First Time

Mark Alderson

CHRISTOPHER, 15 to 17

CHRISTOPHER, *a young teenager wearing a wrinkled T-shirt, is walking in the school hallway with a teenage girl.*

CHRISTOPHER Hey Becky, I've got something to ask you. I know I keep asking you stuff, like "Will you go to homecoming with me?" and "Can I borrow a pencil?" But this time it's different. Also, thanks for saying yes to both of those questions.

I do care about you a lot, and judging by the way you've let me share your straw these past couple of days, I think you care about me too. That's why I want my first everything to be with you.

First kiss? Sure! I was definitely thinking about having that with you. Right now? Um, well I am kind of in the middle of talking to you about something? Can we put "first kiss" on hold?

Where was I? Oh yeah . . . what? You want to hold hands for the first time? Wow, that would be spectacular, except I need both of my hands free to make my point. So can we put a pin in the "first time holding hands thing?" Great. I am almost finished.

I would love for me to take you out on our first date where I pay for the whole thing. I've been working at Bagel Planet all summer just to afford such an occasion. I even have coupons if you'll let me use them.

What's that? Of course I want to walk you to class for the first time! Except, uh, well my next class is Gym and it's on the other side of campus. So how about we put "first walk to class" on hold?

Hey. Becky? Where are you going!? [*A beat, for Becky responding.*] You're right, I should have listened to you the first time. What? Are you sure?

[CHRISTOPHER *hangs his head low.*]

Well, I got what I asked her for. Becky Darlaham was the first girl to dump me. I hope it doesn't hurt as much the second time.

Elevator Action

Jessica Glassberg

CHARLIE, 18

CHARLIE, *wearing a business suit and a wide smile and carrying an oversized briefcase, enters a crowded elevator.*

CHARLIE   Twenty-two please?

[*He looks at the elevator buttons.*]

That's funny, we're all going to 22.

[*A beat. Then,*]

Wait . . . maybe it's just 2? Sorry—can you press 2, please?

[*A beat. Then,*]

Thanks. I'm starting a new job today and I just can't remember the floor. I think I'm just too excited.

[*The door opens. CHARLIE looks around.*]

No, this doesn't look familiar.

[*The door is about to shut.* CHARLIE *pokes his hand between the closing doors and reopens them.*]

But . . . But that hallway . . . That looks familiar. Do the hallways look the same on every floor?

[CHARLIE *stretches his leg back to keep the elevator door open as he looks both ways down the hall. He swings himself back into the elevator.*]

No, it's definitely not 2 . . . I'm a tad dyslexic . . . So maybe it was 5. Can you push 5 for me? Thanks.

I've just never been great with numbers . . . math's never been my thing . . . I don't think there's much math required to be a junior analyst. I hope not. I was always fascinated when a guy in a movie would ask for a girl's number and just remember it. I'd need to write it down . . . Repeat it and make sure I actually got it right and then . . . Oh, here's 5 . . .

[CHARLIE *pokes his head out again.*]

Oh man, I really thought this was going to be it. Sorry. Maybe 6, "6" looks like "5." It's probably 6 . . . Six please. So sorry everyone. I'm just nervous. Nervous and excited to start my life as a businessman. Man, I'm sweating. Can you see that I'm sweating? I hope you can't smell it. Can you smell it?

[*The elevator doors open.*]

[*Nervously laughing:*] Wow, they really do all look so similar. A person could go insane here. Okay. It's not 6. How about 9? Nine is just 6 upside down.

[*He looks at the elevator numbers and turns his head upside down.*]

Yeah. That's gotta be it. The upside-down 6. That looks right.

[*He nervously holds up his cell phone.*]

Does anyone get a signal in here? No? Yeah, I should have double-checked before I left, but I thought I would have remembered. And I wanted to showcase my independence. Sure, my dad got me this job, but I've gotta be the one to keep it, right? I just know this is when everything's going to start coming up Charlie. That's me. I'm Charlie.

[*The elevator doors open.*]

Okay, it's definitely not 9. Who wouldn't remember that mural, right? Are those penguins or skulls? But, I felt really good about 9. So, 19? Let's try 19.

[*Nervously, as if gambling:*] Come on 19. Lucky 19.

[*He laughs awkwardly.*]

Not that I gamble. I mean, I went to one of those Indian casinos once. Is it "Native American" casino? All I do know is that I lost fifty bucks.

[*Looking at his watch:*] Oh man, I'm gonna be late. I don't want to be late on my first day. They don't promote people who are late on their first day. They remember those things.

[*Wringing his hands:*] My hands are so clammy.

[*He wipes his hands on his pants. Seeing they are still clammy, he blows on them.*]

[*Looking at his watch again:*] I really didn't want to be late.

[*Then, realizing:*] Oh no, I'm going to make you all late. I'm so. I'm just so sorry. I'm so stupid.

[*The doors open.*]

I would have remembered that construction.

[CHARLIE *holds his hand in the door and nervously looks back and forth.*]

Can you imagine? I was here three days ago for the interview. I should have just checked the stupid board in the stupid lobby. I'm so stupid. I do this to myself, ya know? That's what my therapist says. I'm worthless. She didn't tell me I'm worthless, but I know I am. Who doesn't write down where they need to go on their first day of work? Who? Charlie Bingham . . . that's who!

[CHARLIE *gets back into the elevator.*]

Okay, I guess I'll head up to 22 and just head back down and check the board. Unless . . . does anyone know where McMillian and Associates is?

[*The elevator doors open.*]

Oh yeah . . . 22. That was it.

[*Reading and acknowledging a giant sign:*] "McMillian and Associates." Looks like I'll see you guys around the watercooler.

Nacho Boyfriend

Kathy S Yamamoto

JOSEPH, early teens

JOSEPH *is an incredibly good-looking young man who, though sometimes dim-witted, is hardworking and means well. His girlfriend, Tabby, broke up with him the day before, after catching him making out with another girl. This is the first time they've seen each other since.*

JOSEPH Hey, hey, hey. Tabby. I know you're mad, but I think I came up with something that will make it better.

[*He pulls out a piece of paper from his pocket and reads from it:*]

Yes, I kissed Annie, Laura, Monica, and Ruth.
I didn't expect for you to find out the truth.

I kissed Ruth last night under the bleachers just so I could make that line rhyme. I missed half of the homecoming game! You should be impressed with my commitment—I mean Ruth is weird. She has that weird eyebrow, and is always talking about her parakeet and the rice at PF Chang's. I mean, I sat through twenty-five minutes of her comparing the rice at PF Chang's to the rice at Kaizuka, before I kissed her. We didn't get back till fifteen minutes after halftime! That's how much I love you, babe.

Although, I guess I could've rhymed "Laura" with "horror," though that's kind of a slant rhyme and I wanted to make sure this was the best poem ever, because I wanted to make it up to my girl.

Wait, don't go! I'm not done. I'm being romantic! Isn't that what you always wanted me to be? To make grand gestures out of being so desperately in love? Well I'm desperate now, baby. Because I know I messed up. And I don't want to lose you. So please? Let me finish?

I know that you're mad and you said that you're leaving,
But you gotta know, you gotta keep believing,
That I love you. And that's what I'm saying,
So please forgive me for all that straying,
And all that straying that I'm bound to do,
Because kissing only one person gets boring,
Even when that one person is you.

Tabby! Come on! That's only the first stanza. Look, I know that you're mad at me, but I'm just trying to be open and honest! I wouldn't mind if you made out with someone else! As long as you did some grand sweeping gesture for me, like make me nachos, but not just regular nachos with shredded cheese—the kind that has pork and jalapenos and tomatoes in it. Like, you could pretty much make out with anybody else if you made that for me. If you made those nachos, I'd even be okay with another dude getting some under-the-shirt action from you.

But if you don't like that idea, that's fine, Tabby. Because I will stop making out with other girls if that's what it takes. I would do anything for you, Tabby. Really, that's why I wrote this poem for you even though I hate poetry, because I want you back. And I worked really hard. I didn't cheat and go on rhymezone.com or anything because that's how much I care about you. I mean, I guess I cheated by cheating on you, but I didn't cheat on the poem. And isn't that the important part? Here, please let me finish.

So I hope that you know that I truly am sorry,
I hope this poem works, 'cause you said you loved them in your diary.

I know, that one is a slant rhyme but I really couldn't help it . . . Not much rhymes with "diary." It's like the "orange" of books. Nothing rhymes with it! Oh yeah, I hope that's okay that I did that, read your diary. I was just getting really desperate and I didn't know what to do. None of your friends would talk to me about it—which was okay, since I felt weird talking to them anyway since I made out with them behind your back.

Although to be fair, Ruth wanted to talk about you, and although that was super helpful, it only added to her being weird. I decided to not talk to her, even though it would've saved me the trouble of reading through your entire diary. Boy, do you write on the toilet a lot? It seems like you do. I guess if I were a girl, I'd write on the toilet too, since it seems like you guys spend so much time on it. You guys are so lucky you get to sit while you pee, that it's socially acceptable. Man, I'd get stuff done on the toilet. Is that why you're so productive, Tabby? Because man, I put off so much other stuff to write this poem, when I could've been doing it on the toilet if I sat to pee. Or if I pooped between the time I felt up Monica and now, which I haven't. Should I see a doctor about that?

Okay fine, fine. Please just let me finish and then if you still feel like you want to dump me, that's fine. I'll just know I did my best.

The moral of this poem is that you are my one,
My other half, I revolve around you like a sun.
And I hope with this poem, your heart I have won,
And if not, I'll just have to hang with my bros,
And find another girl to make me some bomb-ass nachos.

Really? That won't make you stay? Fine. I didn't need you anyway.
Oh my God, I just rhymed, maybe poetry is for me!

Oh no, Ruth. Look, you're very nice but I don't care about the moisture content of PF Chang's rice! I did it again. I'm a genius! No wonder all these girls want me.

Emo Gothic Love

Alessandra Rizzotti

SHAWN, 18

SHAWN *is a tall, skinny guy who is sensitive, full of love, and a lot of darkness. Here, he is hanging out with a girl he likes at the Griffith Park Observatory, at night, with his own telescope. They've been friends for a while, but it just got more serious and he may be taking it more seriously than she is. SHAWN looks through the telescope, up at the sky.*

SHAWN Do you see that? That's Saturn. Cassini is rotating around its rings right now, taking pictures of its surface. Saturn is the flattest planet with the most rings. Seems like a paradox. Like us meeting. We're two depressed people but we somehow make each other happy. But not happy in a sappy way. Just in a normal "here we are, existing" type of way. Cuz you know, being happy is annoying sometimes.

I was really surprised by your text, ya know. I thought I'd have to suppress all my feelings about you and just be your friend, like some kinda gay sidekick. But wow—you thinking I'm attractive? I never feel that way. *You're* the one who's really beautiful, you know? Inside and out—as a person. I didn't think I could open up to anyone this way. My biggest fear is saying too much and seeing you abandon me for that. I feel like a douche canoe for saying that. God, I'm so lame . . . No, I really am.

When you said I could come over when your parents were gone and take a bath, I wanted to take you up on that. Like I really did want to put cucumbers on my face and pretend like I was a woman for a night. I wanted you to paint my nails and tell me stories. Because that felt right. To be with you, vulnerable, in an intimate, raw way. You said I have a feminine power and wow, why not embrace that, right? Is that fucking weird? You know, I've never liked a girl till I met you. I didn't think I could ever do it because my mom is such a bitch that my opinion of women is whatever. I mean, not of you. You're special. But yeah, I've never liked girls. I've never liked guys. I've always just been asexual. You make me feel different, though.

I got out of the house when my mom was yelling at me yesterday just to walk. I never go out. I saw some geese and ducks, said hey what's up, and I was proud of myself for taking that step and seeing the sun and just being my pasty-ass self getting super sunburned. Listening to mariachi by the park and wishing I was Mexican, when I'm just a really tall, feminist machismo man that could be mistaken for a KKK member. God, being in the KKK seems like such an easy thing to do. Great for stupid people to feel like they belong to something. Ha-ha . . . ugh, if only we could feel like we all belonged somewhere, am I right?? It's hard being smart, don't you think? I feel judged a lot. I feel like I'll never amount to anything, when really I have all the potential in the world.

You make me comfortable enough to say that—to admit that I feel inadequate. [*Starts to cry.*] God . . . I'm crying like I'm some kinda emotionally retarded baby. I don't do that in front of people . . . but I feel "myself" around you. I let my guard down and it feels right to embrace that side of me. The entire world crashes in front of my face, but I somehow remain calm knowing I'm here with you.

[*He looks through the telescope.*]

Check it out. Saturn's rings are vibrating through the telescope. It makes me think of holding you tight against my chest. Oh man, here I am crying and all I really want to do is just kiss you. Would you want that? I feel weird asking "Can I kiss you?" because in my mind, we should both want that, at the same time. The gravitational pull between us should be clear, vocally, you know? I feel it, but do you? . . . It's okay. I understand. I should probably stop crying first. I'm such an idiot sometimes. But man, you're wonderful. I'd want to date you if you ever felt like that was something you'd want to do.

You would? Wow. Can I hold your hand right now? I just want to squeeze you.

Phone Drone

JP Karliak

SAM, 13 to 15

SAM *never takes his eyes off his phone, while his dad wants him to pay attention to the world around him. But tonight before dinner, Dad will learn just how aware of the world SAM is.*

SAM Just one second.

[*Beat.*]

Just one second, okay?

[*Beat.*]

Dad, with all due respect, there are, in fact, things I could be doing more important than whatever you have to say. I know that's a crushing blow to your ego . . . I don't mean it to be . . . I'm just saying that governments rise and fall every day regardless of whether we discuss my math homework.

[*Resumes texting.*]

No, I didn't say I'm responsible for government upheaval . . . that'd be crazy, right? . . . I'm just pointing out where our predinner check-in falls on the scale of importance. Not to mention, why can't we talk during dinner like everyone else does? Honestly, I don't mind if you talk with your mouth full.

[*Beat.*]

I can't tell you what I'm doing.

[*Beat.*]

Because I can't.

[*Beat.*]

You can't ground me for that, I have the right to remain silent. Okay, okay—fine. The reason is . . . it's classified.

[*Beat.*]

From who? From everybody, not just you. Wow, your ego is massive, isn't it? Look, there's no reason to panic. When I say "classified," I just mean it's something very important, but completely and utterly harmless.

[*Dad takes the phone.*]

No! A million people will die! I'm serious! And not because I kill them . . . Because I can't save them from imminent, instantaneous destruction unless you give me back my phone.

[*Beat.*]

Yes, "harmless" was a gross understatement! Dad. Please. This is not time to assert your parental power. You have to trust me. Your child. Your flesh and blood, your legacy embodied, the fruit of your good example. You can trust your own child, can't you? Papa Bear?

[*Beat.*]

I don't know who dinged the car door! The phone, Dad. Now!

[*Beat.*]

Okay, fine. Fine. Just know that by saying this now, I'm breaking multiple laws, and I can't guarantee your safety or the safety of this family: I'm a spy.

[*Beat.*]

Yes, a spy. Okay, I recognize it's hard to believe, but I don't think it's funny. Especially not that funny. Please stop laughing.

[*Beat.*]

All right, you want proof? No problem, I'll try to keep this to a minute or less since a million might be dead by then, but here we go:

You and Mom are always on me for too much time on my phone, but every second I spend on it is to protect the life, liberty, and happiness of the American people. Every text is an encoded message with the FBI, CIA, NSA, Homeland Security, and, now and then, even the president. Every tweet, an encrypted instruction to operatives overseas. Every selfie, a facial-recognition scan to access the government's most restricted databases. You think I'm ignoring you listening to indie rock? I'm listening to wiretaps from Beijing. You think I'm launching birds at pigs, I'm launching drone strikes at chemical weapons plants. You think I'm posting my status to Facebook? I'm not. Nobody posts on Facebook anymore.

With every allegedly superficial swipe of who's hot and who's not, I'm actually judging which soldiers are best equipped for a black ops mission. The last time I favorited someone's pic, they got a Congressional Medal of Honor.

Bottom line is that there is too much danger in this world to entrust heroics to every midtwenties cadet fresh out of Langley and West Point. Younger, faster, smarter minds are required to keep the cogs and wheels turning in the complex game of espionage, and I stepped up to the challenge. Believe me, it's not easy facing your parents' constant criticism and disdain, fearing any day you guys might write me off as "our kid who we're pretty sure will live at home long after high school," but that's a risk I'm willing to take if it means you and Mom can sleep safely one more night in a world teetering on the edge.

Now if that sounds more important than my day at school, I'd appreciate you giving me back my phone so I can send a text that will mean hundreds of thousands of other fathers and mothers will survive the night, too. No big deal.

[SAM *gets the phone back.*]

Thanks, Dad. Yeah, we'll talk during dinner.

[SAM *finishes texting. The phone rings. He looks around before answering.*]

Did you receive the transmission?

[*Beat.*]

I know! Her boobs are huge!!

Best Day of My Life So Far

Carla Cackowski

THOMAS, 13

THOMAS *stands in front of a podium addressing his eighth-grade English class. He adjusts the microphone for his height. He is reading aloud an assignment given to him by the teacher.*

THOMAS   Hello, fellow eighth-grade English class students. My name is Thomas Snowden. I'm thirteen years old. I'm here today to read to you from my essay, "Best Day of My Life So Far," based on the topic given to us in this class. Thank you for this opportunity, Mrs. Bricking. You are a kind and conscientious teacher.

[*He reads:*]

The best day of my life so far was the day that I hung out with world leader and president of the United States of America, Barack Obama.

[*Looks to class.*]

It's true. I hung out with him.

[*Back to reading:*]

I won a contest. I never win anything. But this time, I won! My prize for winning this nondescript contest? The president flew me to meet him in Chicago on *Air Force One*! He wanted to hang out in Chicago because he used to live there and stuff. Chicago. The greatest city in all of the United States. Or at least in all of the Midwest.

[*He looks to the teacher.*]

Sorry for all of the exposition, Mrs. Bricking. I'm just trying to give an honest account of my day with the president.

[*Back to reading:*]

First place the president took me was to see a game at Wrigley Field. I noticed that people around us were staring and whispering. They couldn't see Obama. Obama was wearing an invisibility cloak. So I looked like I was talking to myself. Obama said it was nothing personal with the invisibility cloak— he wasn't embarrassed to be seen with me or anything—he just thought there'd be less interruptions this way.

[*To class:*]

Stop snickering, Jacob. The president is a very thoughtful man and has all kinds of technology not available to the general public yet.

[*Back to reading:*]

Next, the president and I took a nice stroll through the Art
Institute. I remarked that an artistic movement would be
named after our president one day. The "Barakque Period."
Then we went in the museum's gift shop, and the president
couldn't stop playing with one of those plastic blocks with
millions of pins that leave an impression of your face when
you push into them. I asked him to pound my first so I could
take a pin imprint of it, as a way of letting future gift-shop
shoppers know that Obama had been there.

[*To teacher:*]

Yes, Mrs. Bricking. I understand that this assignment was
supposed to be a true story. What about my story so far
makes it seem untrue?

[*Back to reading:*]

It'd been such an exciting day and I hadn't had a chance to
take my afternoon nap, so as we sat in the limo on our way
to the next stop, I closed my eyes. President Obama sang me
a lullaby that went something like, "Bahrock oh-bah-mah
baby on the tree top . . ."

[*To class:*]

I'm almost done, you guys. Mrs. Bricking! Please tell them
to be quiet—thank you. You really are a lovely and respected
teacher.

[*Back to reading:*]

When I woke up from my nap, Obama and I were sitting at Buddy Guy's, listening to jazz music and drinking beer.

[*To class:*]

It's true!

[*Reading essay:*]

As we walked to The Wiener's Circle on Clark, I told the president his name sounded like a childhood game I used to play when I would jump over the cracks on the sidewalk singing, "Step on a crack, Bah-rack yo-bam-a-mama's back!"

He handed me my hot dog with extra relish and mustard and I thanked him by saying, "Your name sounds like science: the scientific study of charisma in politicians—Barack Obometry. Your name sounds like a movie with Julia Roberts: Erin Barakovich. A term for passing gas after eating vegetables: Barackoli Obombing. A new position in the Kama Sutra: Ohhh-bomb-uuuuhhh."

[*To teacher:*]

But I'm almost done!

[*Back to essay:*]

As we walked along Lake Michigan, the president pulled off his invisibility cloak and told me it was time for him to get back to the capital. I thanked him for a lovely day. He shook my hand and said, "I had fun too, dude." Then President Barack Obama levitated over the water and floated away. Just like you'd expect from the Dali-Obama.

[*To class:*]

Thank you all for listening.

[*To teacher:*]

Hope I get an A on this one. The president is counting on you, Mrs. Bricking. Don't let him down.

The Mom-Specific Ew

Cooper McHatton

JOHNNY DECKER, 17

JOHNNY *is getting coffee with a friend with whom he'd like to be more than just a friend. As they talk, the subject of* JOHNNY*'s mother comes up.*

JOHNNY   I'm glad you find it great that I love my mother.

I've been told it's sexy when guys love their mother, so it doesn't surprise me. It hits some deep . . . something in women. Some cavewoman response to knowing they are finding a good mate.

[*Beat.*] But . . . it kinda ends right there. My guess is we're likely to have some conflicting ideas.

I bet you're thinking that me loving my mother means that I don't hate her or that I don't forget to give her a card on Mother's Day or her birthday.

My relationship is a little . . . different. My mother and I have a lot in common. We like to hang out.

[*Beat.*]

Yep. There it is. You went "ew."

You see, there is no way any guy can hang with their mother without an ewwww-factor.

Somehow society has decided that it is the biggest red flag in history. It's like I'm immediately destined to be a postal worker with a lot of cats.

But it's only mom-specific.

You see, I can go to a concert with my dad, we can hang out, go get a burger. Talk shop, football, girls, or the latest gadget.

But a guy cannot hang out with his mother to do anything. EVER.

Dinner? Nope.

Oh wait, unless it's her birthday.

Let's just try out a few and see if we can find one . . .

[*Optimistic.*] "I'm going to the movies with my mom."

[*Cheerful.*] "I'm going to a concert with my mom."

[*Gung-ho.*] "I'm going to the beach with my mom."

[*Beat.*]

There's that "ewww."

You can't help it.

You might as well hang a "virgin" tag around my neck and buy me a lot of sweatpants.

The world simply has it out for mothers and sons. Even your grandmother is acceptable, because she's old and you're just being kind, but we are all expected to grow up and away and never look back.

Maybe it's because she's the only nonsexual person in the world who you've ever been held by and laid against while sucking her breasts . . .

[*Beat.*]

Oh, I get it now.

That's it. It's the boobs.

Ew.

Cool with My Dad

Josh Hyman

GREGG, 18

On a humid mid-August day, the university parking lot is full of parents helping their kids move into their first college dorm rooms. Frenetic energy fills the air. Everyone is a little confused, slightly lost, hot and sweaty, highly emotional, and trying to keep themselves together. GREGG, a freshman and the oldest of his siblings, watches his father drive off after he has helped his son move in. But there are a few things that GREGG's forgotten to say. He calls his father's cell phone, but it goes straight to voicemail.

GREGG Hey, Dad. I'm standing here in the parking lot watching you . . . speed . . . through that red light. Nice. Anyway, I just wanted to leave you a message and say thanks for the ride. And for helping me move into my first dorm room. And for greasing my palm, too. I'm sure this extra five dollars will land me a ton of . . . gum.

I also want you to know, I saw you crying as you got into the car. Its okay, Dad. You did good.

Look, I don't want to be sappy, but do you remember when you and I would just dance? Not like at my bar mitzvah with Grandpa or at Lilah's wedding, but when you and I were alone, like in the living room at our house, and there was a Michael Jackson song on the radio, or a new James Taylor CD you bought? We would do our little dancey-jiggy-hop thing. You'd do that subtle boogie, shoulder's popping up and down, with a little knee-bend bop . . . like an old man grooving to the oldies . . . just dancing to your own tune? It was awesome . . . so much fun. And if we were in the car, you'd play the piano on the dashboard or on my head . . . even if there wasn't a piano in the song. I'm sure lots of dads do that . . . but I got to do it with you, my dad. Well, for three years, anyway, until Brad came along. And then two years later, when Carrie arrived. I guess my sharing skills have been thrown into full effect since then, but for those first three years, I was your number one dance partner, your sole proprietor with exclusive ownership rights, and I'm just saying, I cherish those times.

But what's funny is, when I got older and saw you dance like that, I used to laugh and say you were being uncool. Eventually I grew to think you were a dork and even at times became embarrassed to be around you.

Like, I'm sure you remember, but I'd say things like, "Dad! Please, don't tell that story!! Nobody wants to hear about your new Internet friends."

Or, "Dad, stop calling my friends "queer-ducks"—to their
face—they think you don't like them." . . .
And then you would say, "I DON'T like them!"
And then I would say, "I KNOW! Just, shush!"

But what you were doing couldn't have been any "more
cool." You were just being silly, which is to say, you were
being confident enough to laugh at your own expense, and
that's all you were ever trying to do. Make people
chuckle . . . especially me.

Now I know you liked to mess with us, too. I mean, the end
of every pep talk or life lesson or scolding would consist of
some kind of contradictory prose, like,
"Sometimes the going gets tough, and sometimes you're a
loser."

I'd be like, "Uhhh, huh? I don't . . . get . . . it!?"

Or remember that time Brad was trying to come up with a
game plan for getting our neighbor Alyse to like him back.
Your advice was,
"You can't make snow on a sixty-degree day!"
. . . and I was like, "How is that supposed to help him!"

I believe your advice on making good decisions was,
"Ya see, the world spins round and round and sometimes
the winds blow north to south . . . but there's only so much
good you could do if it's not something that you should!"

I'll never forget Mom looking down at me and whispering,
" . . . if a woodchuck, could chuck, wood!"

My favorite though, was,
"Have fun! Be careful! And don't forget, you're
insignificant."

Now, I know, I know you weren't trying to be mean or
hurtful—just trying to tell us to not let life bum us out . . .
that the world doesn't revolve around us, so don't make a big
deal about little things! Of course, all I heard at the time
was, "You have no purpose, shithead!" I'm a fifteen-year-
old-boy and all I know is, I can't get girls AND my dad
thinks I'm a tool bucket! But your brilliance was that it
brought us together. You and me. A joke at my expense or
yours, but exclusively for us. A laugh we can always share.

I just hadn't realized it before, but what you were doing was
protecting me, because all you cared about was making me
be better. Well I'm telling you now, it worked. You were,
you are, and you will always be my master mold—my
ultimate motivator. I don't care how others perceive you,
because to me, you're always going to be the coolest guy I
know. You taught me how to dress, how to see the world,
how to talk to girls, and how to withhold yourself from
killing your kids when they're putting the car into reverse,
crashing it into the family mailbox. I mean, the restraint you
displayed that day was greek in its artistry. But by showing
me the ropes, Dad, you were being cool with me, saying,

"You're my pal . . . you're my boy . . . now go out into the world . . . and don't make me look stupid."

I just wanted you to know that I understand. And seeing you drive off right now, seeing you shed a few man-tears, I know you know it too. I'm just saying, Dad, any time you want to debate some crazy topic, like "Why time doesn't really exist," or argue over how much the Mets suck, or just sit around and tell each other joke-book jokes, then I'm game. Any time and every time. Because that's cool. And when we connect on something funny or when one of us introduces the other to a new song we both dig, then let's dance about it. Because those moments, of being cool with my dad, are mine and mine alone. Forever.

Just wanted you to know that . . . as you peel out on the highway like a maniac. Drive safely, please. And when that campus police officer you passed pulls you over, just do me a favor? If he asks who you think you are . . . tell him you're my dad. Then tell him he's insignificant.

Love you.

Oh, you're calling me back right now. Okay, here we go. Ahem.

"Hey Dad . . ."

Contributors

ALISHA GADDIS is a Latin Grammy Award–winning performer, Emmy-nominated actress, humorist, writer, and producer based in Los Angeles. She is a graduate of New York University's Tisch School of the Arts and the University of Sydney, Australia.

Alisha's first book, *Women's Comedic Monologues That Are Actually Funny*, was published by Hal Leonard/Applause Books in 2014. Subsequently, she signed on with Hal Leonard to release five more books in this series, which includes the book you are currently holding in your hands. Her columns have appeared in College Candy, Comediva, *GOOD* magazine, and Thought Catalog. Alisha is the founder and head writer of Say Something Funny . . . B*tch!—the nationally acclaimed all-female online magazine. The highly irreverent Messenger Card line that she cofounded and writes for is sold in boutiques nationally.

Alisha currently stars in the TV show she cocreated and executive produced, *Lishy Lou and Lucky Too*, as part of the Emmy Award–winning children's series *The Friday Zone* on PBS/PBS KIDS.

Alongside her husband, Lucky Diaz, she is the cofounder and performer for Latin Grammy Award–winning Lucky Diaz and the Family Jam Band. Their children's music has topped the charts at Sirius XM and is *People* magazine's No. 1 album of the year—playing Los Angeles Festival of Books, Target Stage, the Smithsonian, the Getty Museum, Madison Square Park, Legoland, New York City's Symphony Space, and more. Their song "Falling" has been used in Coca-Cola's summer national ad campaign.

As a stand-up comic and improviser, Alisha has headlined the nation at the World Famous Comedy Store and the New York Comedy Club, and has been named one of the funniest upcoming female comics by *Entertainment Weekly*. As a performer, she has appeared on Broadway; has performed at the Sydney Opera House, Second City Hollywood, Improv Olympic West, Upright Citizens Brigade, and the Comedy Central Stage; and has toured with her acclaimed solo shows *Step-Parenting: The Last Four Letter Word* and *The Search for Something Grand*. She has also appeared on MTV, CBS, CNN, Univision, NBC, A&E, and has voiced many national campaigns. Alisha is a proud SAG-AFTRA, NARAS, LARAS, and AEA member.

She loves her husband the most.

www.alishagaddis.com

JEFF BOGLE The exoskeleton of teenage Jeff has long since been shed, but the sarcastic, highly independent boy is alive and well inside his adult incarnation. Instead of listening to hair bands and writing bad poetry, Jeff has spent the better part of his thirties writing and podcasting about fatherhood, travel, and

All Things Childhood on his site, Out With The Kids (OWTK).
He thinks it's rad that his work frequently appears on the
Huffington Post and PBS. No one would be more surprised
than teenage Jeff to learn that an adorable redheaded gal saw
fit to marry him, and that together they've spawned a pair of
hilarious, strange, and lovely young ladies. Jeff considers himself one of the most fortunate guys in the world, although he
often needs to be reminded of this fact. Ideally, Jeff would climb
the tallest mountain and scream THANK YOU to Alisha for
including him in this absurdly funny book, but in lieu of that,
there's this final sentence of a bio that's already over word-count.
OWTK.com

CARLA CACKOWSKI is a person who does things. She
toured the world performing comedy (on a boat!) with comedy
troupe the Second City, and she currently teaches improvisa-
tion to wonderful dreamers at the the Second City in Los
Angeles. Carla has written and performed five comedic solo
shows that have played in superfun places like Los Angeles,
New York City, San Diego, and Austin. She's a member of the
Solo Collective, a theater company currently in residence at
VS. Theater in Los Angeles. Her monologues were published
in the previous anthologies *Women's Comedic Monologues That
Are Actually Funny* (Applause Books, 2014) and *Men's Comedic
Monologues That Are Actually Funny* (Applause Books, 2015).
She is a member of SAG-AFTRA and, as a voice-over artist,
has been featured on television shows such as *iCarly*, *Pretty
Little Liars*, and *Cougar Town*. Carla was head writer on *Lishy*

Lou and Lucky Too, an adorably hilarious children's show that aired on PBS KIDS. Carla really loves her family and friends and hopes that even if she never procreates, two hundred years from now someone will think of her when they read her monologues in these books.

www.carlacackowski.com

AMBER COLLINS-PARNELL grew up in Los Angeles. She is a student at the University of Chicago and majors in cinema and media studies. Her most recent work includes "The Image: An Underrated Construct" as well as other various essays analyzing film. She currently lives in Chicago.

HANNAH GANSEN is a Los Angeles–based comedian, writer, and singer-songwriter. She has performed at numerous festivals (Fringe, Women in Comedy, Hollywood, L.A. Comedy), clubs (Laugh Factory, Comedy Central Stage, Comedy Store, the Apollo, Zanie's, the Improv, IO West, IO Chicago, Flappers, the Ice House), and underground/alternative comedy venues. Her music/comedy album, *Al the Bum*, is available on iTunes and Amazon.

www.hannahgansen.com

JESSICA GLASSBERG is a comedy writer and stand-up comedian. For ten years, she was the head writer on *The Jerry Lewis MDA Telethon* and performed stand-up on the nationally syndicated show five times. She has also written for Disney XD, "A Hollywood Christmas at The Grove" for *Extra*, and the Screen Actors Guild Awards (where her jokes were highlighted on E!'s *The Soup*, EntertainmentWeekly.com, and Hollywood.com). Additionally, Jessica was a featured performer on *The History of the Joke with Lewis Black* on the History Channel. Her monologues have also been published in the books *Women's Comedic Monologues That Are Actually Funny* and *Men's Comedic Monologues That Are Actually Funny*. She currently produces and hosts a stand-up comedy showcase in Los Angeles called "Laugh, Drink, Repeat." Jessica is also a prolific digital writer, with her work featured on HelloGiggles.com, Reductress.com, HotMomsClub.com, Kveller.com, AbsrdComedy.com, and Torquemag.io. For upcoming shows, clips, and writing samples, follow her on twitter at http://twitter.com/JGlassberg.

www.jessicaglassberg.com

ANDY GOLDENBERG knows that bios are super boring. You don't care where he's from (Florida) or where he got his theater diploma (University of Miami). You want to know how he's famous. He played Adam Sandler's acting double and scene partner in *Jack and Jill* (2011): when Adam played Jack, Andy played Jill. His Goldentusk YouTube channel has more than 50 million views, with *Time Out New York* film critic Keith Uhlich nicknaming him the Theme Song Sondheim. He was a coverboy of the *Nice Jewish Guys Calendar*, wrote and performed sketch comedy with *National Lampoon*'s Lemmings Sketch Troupe, published a children's book called *Peter, the Paranoid Pumpkin*. You can look up his television and film work, because he doesn't want you to be lazy. You think you're an amazing actor? Try and perform this bio for your next audition.

www.youtube.com/goldentusk

DEREK HEEREN is a mild-mannered businessman by day and sleep enthusiast by night. Between all that sleeping and business-ing, he is an actor, a writer, and an award-winning editor (awarded from a small film festival in 2002, but I still count it!). From the age of nine, Derek began writing (but not finishing) a variety of short stories, novels, and homework assignments (a proud tradition that he continues to this day). Derek hails from Bloomington, MN, and went to college in St. Paul, MN, where he graduated with a BA in theatre arts from Bethel College (which has, itself, now graduated to Bethel *University*). Currently, he lives in Los Angeles with his wife and two-year-old daughter, who both give him endless joy and writing material.

JOSH HYMAN is a New York City–based actor, comedian, and writer. He studied at the Atlantic Acting School, performs stand-up comedy and improv on stages all around the city, and has competed in numerous IFNY Monologue Slam competitions, winning the Battle of the Champions in 2011. He is also known for his commercial TV work, appearing in spots for Dunkin' Donuts, Time Warner Cable, AT&T, ESPN, Jimmy Dean, Lowe's, Verizon FiOS, Bud Light, and more. Josh is also an original cast member of the Off-Broadway smash-hit

Drunk Shakespeare, and has also appeared on CBS's *Blue Bloods* and Nick Jr.'s *Team Umizoomi*. Along with developing the TV pilot *Sport Smart* and the web series *Let's Shoot Dirty*, he also produces YouTube videos—most notably the *You Down With JPP* song-parody sensation that accompanied the New York Giants' 2012 Super Bowl run. For more, visit YouTube/MrJoshHyman and Instagram/Twitter @MrJoshHyman. *MrJoshHyman.com*

JP KARLIAK Voice-over artist, writer, solo performer, and snappy dresser, JP hails from the "Electric City" Scranton, PA. His voice has fallen out of the mouths of Marvel heroes and villains, a werewolf nemesis of the *Skylanders*, and the self-proclaimed supergenius Wile E. Coyote, among others. On screen, he planned a fancy party for Sarah Michelle Gellar and delivered singing telegrams to *The Real Husbands of Hollywood*. A graduate of the USC School of Theatre, iO West, and Second City Training Center, he has written numerous short films and plays produced in locales around the country. His full-length solo show, *Donna/Madonna*, has garnered awards at the United Solo, New York International Fringe, and San Francisco Fringe Festivals. He can always be found at fancy chocolate boutiques or on his website. *jpkarliak.com*

BRENDAN McCAY is an actor/writer/comedian originally from sunny and delightful Phoenix, AZ. After studying communication and theatre at Northern Arizona University,

Brendan started performing improv and sketch comedy at National Comedy Theatre Phoenix. He has since moved to Los Angeles, where he completed the iO West training program and the Second City Hollywood Conservatory. Brendan currently writes and performs with the sketch team Raffle at iO West. Having had an awkward yet entertaining adolescence, he is honored to be making his writing debut in this compilation of *Teen Boys' Comedic Monologues That Are Actually Funny*. He thanks his wife, Brittany, for her constant support and her continuous patience with his tomfoolery.

www.brendanmccay.com

COOPER McHATTON is a self-proclaimed tech and pop-culture geek. He cocreated Playfic, a website for writing and playing interactive fiction that has been used as a teaching tool at numerous high schools and colleges around the country. He occasionally performs as a professional puppeteer operating big furry monsters in a family rock-music spectacular. Cooper contributes frequently to family and pop-culture blogs, magazines, and websites. He is known to be a fine curator of amazing things with small, devoted followings. Having never spent a day in a traditional school setting until he entered college at age sixteen, he never had the pleasure of experiencing wedgies or swirlies or any other types of torment, and is pleasantly delusional. He's currently a math and comedy nerd and is convinced the two are completely intertwined. Cooper is your typical, ordinary, everyday joyful overachiever. He's a vegetarian, an activist, a pacifist, and a ghost pepper connoisseur.

He resides in sunny Southern California, which might explain his constant, overly happy disposition.

cooperdiem.com

KATE McKINNEY is a writer, performer, and social-media maven from Southern Indiana. In spring of 2015 she co-produced and codirected the show *Listen to Your Mother* for Evansville, IN. She writes the blog *Mammacake*, and gleans her comic inspiration from her four hilarious children. Kate realized she was funny the day she stopped taking herself so seriously! Her piece in this book was based on conversations with her husband, Hugh McKinney, cowriter of the piece, who is called "the funniest man on Facebook" by his friends. Follow her @katecake.

www.katharinemckinney.com

KIM MULLIGAN is a comedic artist in Los Angeles. She was raised in the Bronx, NY, and Nashua, NH, which may explain her dry humor and addiction to hoodies. She loves sci-fi, especially the *Buffy* series and *Doctor Who*. Her humor is quirky, smart, and a bit dark. Kim graduated with a BFA from Massachusetts College of Art and Design at age twenty-one, married her high school sweetheart at twenty-two, then moved to Southern California where it's pretty and there's never snow to shovel! She loves producing edgy live comedy shows, particularly with husband and creative partner, Andy Bouley. Both studied sketch at Upright Citizens Brigade. Kim and Andy perform under their "celebrity" name KAndy, and have written, directed, performed, and taken the blame for hundreds of live shows—many at iO West where Kim went through the improv training program. They also make comedy videos, including the *Holiday Hooker* series, which has an Immortal video on *Funny or Die* and *Folgers Fail*, featured on *Tosh.0*. Kim has formed multiple award-winning sketch teams and has performed at many improv and sketch festivals internationally. She's performed at iO West, the Comedy Central Stage, Upright Citizens Brigade, the Improv, the Comedy Store, and Second City.

@getsomekandy

GINA NICEWONGER has been "writing in the moment" by performing improv comedy for over ten years. She has written and performed in shows at the Annoyance Theater and Improv Olympic in Chicago and, more recently, at various theaters throughout Los Angeles. In addition to monologues published here and in *Men's Comedic Monologues That Are Actually Funny*, Gina wrote one-acts produced by Studio C Artists and enjoys writing sketch comedy with the groups BBQ Committee, Chrissy and Gina, and Hot Lunch. When not making stuff up, Gina enjoys teaching elementary school.

CHRIS QUINTOS is a writer/actor/housewife who is lucky enough to live in both San Francisco and Los Angeles. She loves being right, hanging out with her dog—Beta, shopping in bulk, and books. She dislikes scary movies, walking on sidewalk grates, cleaning her car, and clowns. She'd like to thank her husband for being wonderful and handsome (AND VERY PATIENT). Many thanks to her family and friends who let her be 1,000 percent Chris, whatever that means. Thanks also to Alisha Gaddis for being a kick-ass lady. She cannot believe she is being published in a book—an actual book! Follow, stalk, chat @chrisquintos.

www.chrisquintos.com

RACHEL RAINES grew up in St. Louis, where she spent time working in the performing arts and volunteering in theater. She attended the American Musical and Dramatic Academy in California, studying film and stage acting as well as being trained in improvisational comedy. She has worked as a free-lance writer for seven years, and her past work includes an essay in *The Diamond Project: Ordinary Women Leading Extraordinary Lives*, edited by: Cynthia Hurst, and various articles for online social media. She currently lives in Los Angeles.

ALESSANDRA RIZZOTTI has written for *GOOD*, *Heeb*, *Smith*, *Hello Giggles*, and *The Neave*. She's also been published in three Harper Perennial books with her six-word memoirs, and is now working on a novel about finding her father. She currently edits for *Backstage Magazine*, bridging the gap between filmmakers and actors.

Alessandrarizzotti.com

MEG SWERTLOW was born and raised in Los Angeles. She left the City of Angels to attend Hamilton College in Clinton,

NY. Meg then came home from the village of Clinton to study and perform comedy. Training at the Groundlings, UCB, and iO West, she's performed improv and stand-up all over the country, even writing her own one-woman show, *The Irresponsible Girl's Guide to Dating*, which she is turning into a book. After a series of increasingly odd jobs, Meg landed a "grown-up" job and began working for *Entertainment Tonight* and *The Insider* as a web producer. She was there for four years before leaving to be a blogger for *X17online* and *Wonderwall*, where she found an abundance of material writing about Kim Kardashian's butt until Lorne Michaels plucked her from obscurity and put her on *SNL*. Hey, it's possible—stranger things have happened—like Stonehenge. And yes, if you must know, the monologue she wrote is pretty much about her ex-boyfriend.

KATHY YAMAMOTO is a Los Angeles native, although she wishes she had been born in Warsaw, Poland. She could've been born in Poland, but her dad made her mom immigrate before her birth so she might one day be president. From an early age, she realized she had a knack for making others laugh, even earning the title of "Funniest Girl in Traditional Japanese Dance Class," an honor admittedly earned without much competition. Now instead of governing the free world, Kathy spends her time writing and performing comedy. In addition to performing improv and stand-up around town, Kathy is a writer on iO West's topical sketch team, Top Story Weekly. You can find her on YouTube in her web series, *Kat&Nat*, and on Twitter @yamaDRAMA.

Acknowledgments

THANKS

A lot of people are awesome. Some people are more awesome in regards to this book. They get extra thanks from Alisha Gaddis:

Thank you to Sara Camilli—best literary agent ever. I adore you. You are like family to me. And look—now we have a series! And like you always say, "This is just the beginning!"

Thank you to all the writers. You all put yourselves out there. It is hard to be funny, and extra super hard to be funny on paper in a particular format. You guys did it, and it is amazing!

Thank you to Hal Leonard and Applause Acting Series (especially John Cerullo and Marybeth Keating). You guys have given me so much guidance, support, and freedom. I couldn't ask for more in a publisher. Thank you to Patty Hammond, the copyeditor of awesome. You make all our funny ramblings readable and grammatically perfect. We ALL thank you for that.

Thank you to my parents, family, and friends. Obviously. You all are the best.

Thank you to my self-titled "personal assistant," Ella Diaz. You are an awesome stepdaughter, and—as promised—when this is published I owe you a macaroon.

And the super biggest thanks of all to my handsome husband, Lucky Diaz. You are my ideal match. Thank you for inspiring me to live past my largest, most grand dream. You make me better every single day. I cannot thank you enough. But I will keep trying.

Other Monologue and Scene Books

Best Contemporary Monologues for Kids Ages 7-15
edited by Lawrence Harbison
9781495011771 ....$16.99

Best Contemporary Monologues for Men 18-35
edited by Lawrence Harbison
9781480369610 ....$16.99

Best Contemporary Monologues for Women 18-35
edited by Lawrence Harbison
9781480369627 ....$16.99

Best Monologues from The Best American Short Plays, Volume Three
edited by William W. Demastes
9781480397408 ....$19.99

Best Monologues from The Best American Short Plays, Volume Two
edited by William W. Demastes
9781480385481 ....$19.99

Best Monologues from The Best American Short Plays, Volume One
edited by William W. Demastes
9781480331556 ....$19.99

Childsplay
A Collection of Scenes and Monologues for Children
edited by Kerry Muir
9780879101886 ....$16.99

Duo!
The Best Scenes for Two for the 21st Century
edited by Joyce E. Henry, Rebecca Dunn Jaroff, and Bob Shuman
9781557837028 ....$19.99

Duo!
Best Scenes for the 90's
edited by John Horvath, Lavonne Mueller, and Jack Temchin
9781557830302 ....$18.99

In Performance
Contemporary Monologues for Men and Women Late Teens to Twenties
by JV Mercanti
9781480331570 ....$18.99

In Performance
Contemporary Monologues for Men and Women Late Twenties to Thirties
by JV Mercanti
9781480367470 ....$16.99

The Monologue Audition
A Practical Guide for Actors
by Karen Kohlhaas
9780879102913 ....$22.99

One on One
The Best Men's Monologues for the 21st Century
edited by Joyce E. Henry, Rebecca Dunn Jaroff, and Bob Shuman
9781557837011 ....$18.99

One on One
The Best Women's Monologues for the 21st Century
edited by Joyce E. Henry, Rebecca Dunn Jaroff, and Bob Shuman
9781557837004 ....$18.99

One on One: Playing with a Purpose
Monologues for Kids Ages 7-15
edited by Stephen Fife and Bob Shuman with contribuing editors Eloise Rollins-Fife and Marit Shuman
9781557838414 ....$16.99

One on One: The Best Monologues for Mature Actors
edited by Stephen Fife
9781480360198 ....$19.99

Scenes and Monologues of Spiritual Experience from the Best Contemporary Plays
edited by Roger Ellis
9731480331563 ....$19.99

Scenes and Monologues from Steinberg/ATCA New Play Award Finalists, 2008–2012
edited by Bruce Burgun
9781476868783 ....$19.99

Soliloquy!
The Shakespeare Monologues
edited by Michael Earley and Philippa Keil
9780936839783 Men's Edition ...$11.95
9780936839790 Women's Edition ...$14.95

Teen Boys' Comedic Monologues That Are Actually Funny
edited by Alisha Gaddis
9781480396791 ....$14.99

Women's Comedic Monologues That Are Actually Funny
edited by Alisha Gaddis
9781480360426...............$14.99

APPLAUSE
THEATRE & CINEMA BOOKS
AN IMPRINT OF
HAL•LEONARD®

Prices, contents, and availability subject to change without notice.